HOME PLUMBING

BLACK CAT

W 126836

This edition published in 1988 by Black Cat, an imprint of
Macdonald & Co (Publishers) Ltd, Greater London House,
Hampstead Road, London NW1

A Pergamon Press plc company

ISBN 0-7481-0076-8

Printed by Henri Proost & Cie Pvba, Belgium

CONTENTS

TYPES OF PIPEWORK

Lead and iron are no longer used as plumbing materials, having been replaced by copper or stainless steel. Now plastic pipework is revolutionising domestic plumbing.

Virtually all **soil pipes** are now made from UPVC (1), which can be joined together using solvent welds or ring seals. Likewise, **overflow pipes** (2) are also made from UPVC, and lengths of these are connected with push-fit joins.

Waste pipes, made of UPVC and ABS plastic, are used for taking water away from baths, basins and sinks (3). Depending on the system they can be joined either by solvent welding or push-fit connections.

Plastic can also be used for water supply pipes. **Polybutylene pipes** (4) can take hot and cold water, the pipes being joined by compression fittings or special push-fit connectors. Similarly, **CPVC pipe** (5) can be used for hot and cold runs, but this is joined with solvent welds.

Black **polythene pipe** (6), the first plastic pipe to be used generally in domestic plumbing, is only suitable for cold water supplies, and consequently is mainly employed for garden and other outside water services.

Rainwater downpipes (7) are made from UPVC and have either circular or square profiles.

Half-hard temper **copper pipe** (8) is used for hot and cold distribution and central heating pipes, being easy to bend and join. **Stain-less steel** (9) has also been used, mainly because it can be joined to copper and galvanised steel without causing electrolytic action.

Flexible copper pipe (10), which can be bent simply in the hands, is ideal for making the awkward connections between tap tails and the supply pipes without having to alter the existing runs.

UNDERSTANDING WATER SUPPLY

Each one of us uses about 160 litres (35 gallons) of water a day, and takes it for granted. Only in a long spell of dry weather comes an awareness that we should use it carefully. Our use is controlled by the supply system – this is how it works.

In the last 50 years the consumption of water has almost doubled. Rising standards of living have given rise to increased consumption, and a greater awareness of the need for hygiene has also played a large role in increasing the demand. Faced with this high demand, supply sources have been hard pressed to keep up.

Where it comes from

Water is supplied by the local water authority (or the 'Undertaking' as it is known in the plumbing trade). After falling as rain it is collected in reservoirs which are fed by streams and rivers, or is pumped from underground wells. Water varies a lot in its chemical makeup since it picks up minerals and gases as it flows. If it picks up calcium, magnesium and sodium salts it will be 'hard' – the menace of pipe systems. Before being distributed it is usually filtered through sand and pebble beds to remove solids and organisms, and may have chlorine added to it to ensure that it is 'potable' – drinkable. Fluoride is also sometimes added for the protection of teeth.

Distribution is carried out by a network of pipes starting with 'trunk mains' which may be as much as 610mm (24in) in diameter. These split into mains and sub-mains which run underneath streets and side streets. It is these sub-mains which are tapped by individual houses for their supply.

The house system may be 'direct' in which all cold water supplies are piped direct from the rising main, with the cistern only being used to supply the hot water tank. Or it may be an 'indirect' system in which all cold-water supplies are taken from the cistern, with the exception of a direct supply to the kitchen sink for drinking purposes.

For water to flow through the trunk mains – and eventually into your house – it must be under a certain amount of pressure. This pressure is assisted by pumps but it is vital that somewhere in the mains system the water should reach a height in a reservoir or water tower, higher than any domestic system it has to supply. The vertical distance through which the water 'falls' is known as the 'pressure head' and without it our

cisterns would never fill up without a lot of expensive additional pumping. The storage cistern also provides a pressure head inside the house, which is why it's preferable to have it in the roof space.

The house system

The sub-main underneath the road is tapped by the 'communication pipe' which ends at the authority's stop-valve. This is usually situated under the pavement about 300mm (1ft) outside the boundary of your property. The stop-valve is located at the bottom of a vertical 'guard' pipe – about 1 metre (39in) deep – which is covered at the surface by a hinged metal cover. It should only be operated by the water authority and requires a special key to turn it. But in a real emergency you may be able to turn it yourself. In old houses it may be the only way of turning off the water supply. After this stop-valve the water enters the service pipe and from then on all pipes become your responsibility.

The service pipe continues under the wall of the property at a depth of at least 750mm (2ft 6in) to protect it from frost – though some water authorities insist that it should be 900mm (3ft) deep. As it travels under the house wall or foundation it usually goes through an earthenware pipe to protect it

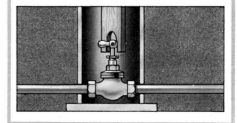
5

INDIRECT COLD SUPPLY

The most common system of water supply in the UK is called 'indirect' because most taps take water from the storage cistern in the roof and not direct from the mains. The cistern is fed by the rising main which in turn is fed by the distribution pipe from the mains.

Water input to the cistern is controlled by a high pressure ball-valve. If this valve jams open the water level rises to flow out of the overflow or 'warning' pipe which should stick well out from the wall.

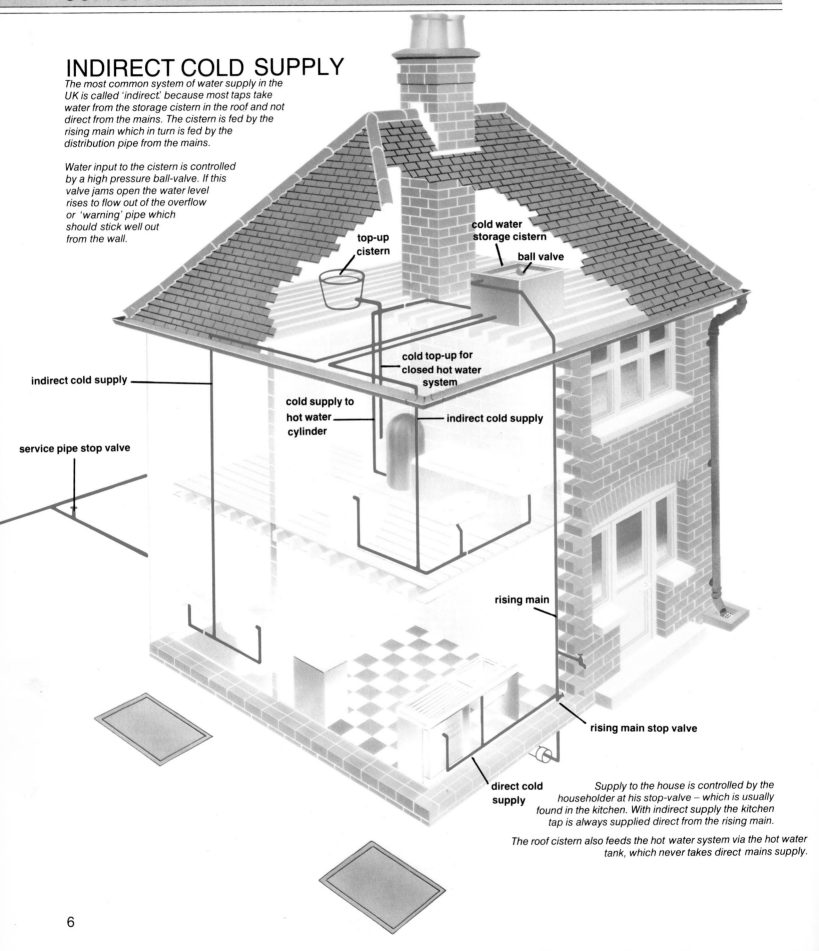

top-up cistern

cold water storage cistern

ball valve

cold top-up for closed hot water system

indirect cold supply

cold supply to hot water cylinder

indirect cold supply

service pipe stop valve

rising main

rising main stop valve

direct cold supply

Supply to the house is controlled by the householder at his stop-valve – which is usually found in the kitchen. With indirect supply the kitchen tap is always supplied direct from the rising main.

The roof cistern also feeds the hot water system via the hot water tank, which never takes direct mains supply.

from possible settlement which might cause it to fracture. To prevent any risk of freezing in cold weather the service pipe should not emerge above ground level until it is at least 600mm (2ft) inside the inside wall surface.

Up to about 40 years ago, service pipes were usually made of lead (in fact the word plumbing originally stemmed from the Latin word for lead – *plumbum).* Today copper and polythene are used instead. The latter is particularly good as it is a poor conductor of heat and is less prone to freezing and fracture.

The service pipe

The service pipe continues under the wall near the kitchen sink, which means that it is often attached to the inner face of the outside wall. This is contrary to the recommendation that it should be attached to an inside wall, and so such a pipe should be lagged with insulation material. The pipe should also be insulated if it comes through any sub-ground floor cavity where it would be subjected to the icy blasts of winter from under-floor ventilation. Again these pre-cautions are both intended to minimise the risk of frost damage.

When the service pipe rises above the ground floor it is called the 'rising main' and it eventually terminates in the supply cistern, which is usually in the roof cavity. The house-holder's main stop-valve is usually found on the rising main a little way above floor level. This is the most important 'tap' in the house. In any plumbing emergency – when bursts or leaks occur, for example, your first action should be to turn this tap off, thus isolating the house system from the mains water supply. The stop-valve should always be turned off when you go away if the house is going to be empty. In old houses the location of the stop-valve may vary considerably, it may be in the cellar, under the stairs, or even under a cover beneath the front path – or it may not exist at all, in which case the authority's stop-valve is the only control.

Branch supply pipes

At least one 'branch' supply pipe leaves the rising main close above the stop-valve and drain tap – this is to the tap over the kitchen sink. This tap must be supplied direct from the main supply as it is supposed to provide all drinking and cooking water. Water which has been in a storage cistern is no longer considered drinkable, sometimes termed 'potable', as it may be slightly contaminated by debris in the storage cistern.

Other branches may be taken at this point to an outside tap, or to a washing machine or dishwasher.

The rising main continues upwards and while its ultimate destination is the cold water storage cistern the pipework in between will vary from house to house, depending on

OTHER SYSTEMS

Other systems
There are other sorts of supply systems both for hot and cold water – and many variations. Systems reflect the design of buildings and the regulations.

Direct cold supply
The direct cold water system takes water direct from the main to all cold water taps. A roof storage cistern is still used but only as a supply reservoir for the hot water tank. Not only the main cistern but also all WC cisterns must have high pressure valves. The indirect system has the advantage of relieving the piping of high pressures and providing a temporary reserve in periods of drought when supplies may be restricted.

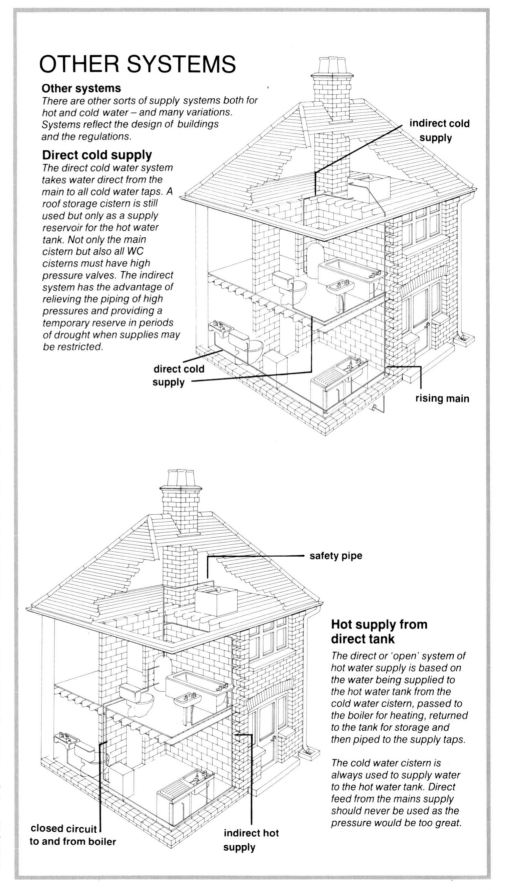

indirect cold supply

direct cold supply

rising main

safety pipe

Hot supply from direct tank

The direct or 'open' system of hot water supply is based on the water being supplied to the hot water tank from the cold water cistern, passed to the boiler for heating, returned to the tank for storage and then piped to the supply taps.

The cold water cistern is always used to supply water to the hot water tank. Direct feed from the mains supply should never be used as the pressure would be too great.

closed circuit to and from boiler

indirect hot supply

INDIRECT HOT WATER SUPPLY

In an indirect or 'closed' hot water system a closed pipe runs from the boiler, through a heat exchanger in the hot water tank and back to the boiler again. This closed system contains water which never comes into contact with the hot water used by the household. The closed circuit between boiler and hot water cylinder loses water very slowly, and is topped up automatically by water from a small reservoir cistern in the loft. A safety pipe returns over-heated water to this or the main cistern.

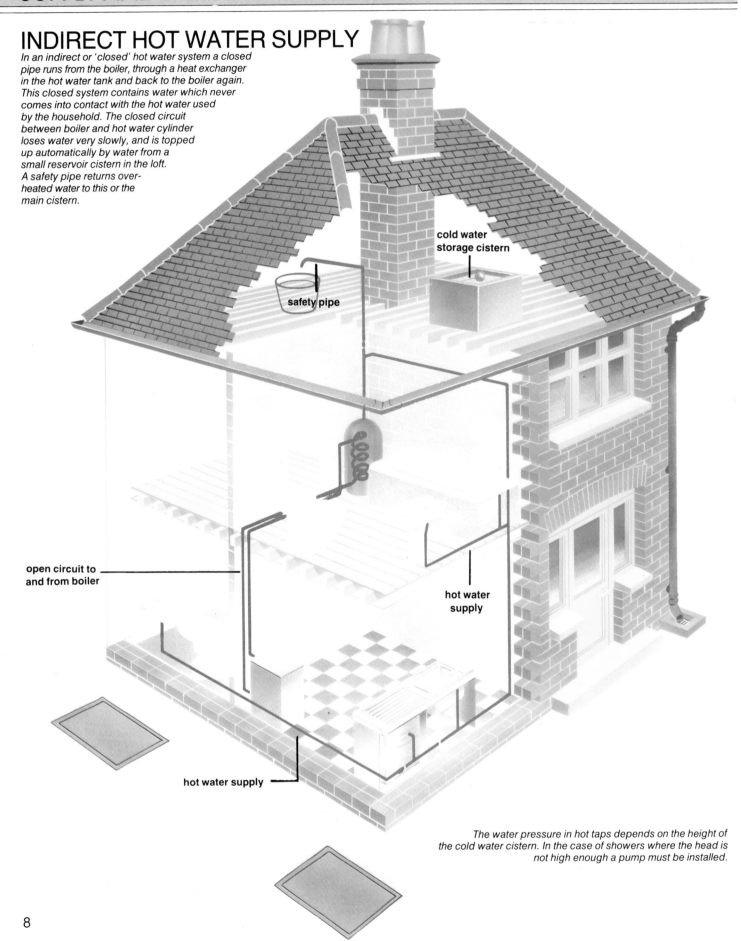

cold water storage cistern

safety pipe

open circuit to and from boiler

hot water supply

hot water supply

The water pressure in hot taps depends on the height of the cold water cistern. In the case of showers where the head is not high enough a pump must be installed.

whether a 'direct' or 'indirect' system has been installed.

In many areas indirect systems must be installed in new buildings, yet in Western Europe direct systems are the rule. Indirect systems have been encouraged because of the difficulty in maintaining constant mains pressure particularly at times of peak demand. Routing of most supplies through the storage cistern evens out fluctuations, and it also rules out the risk of 'back siphonage' whereby dirty water could be sucked back into the mains supply – though this rarely occurs. The 1976 drought in the UK provided good reason for indirect systems, since each house had an emergency supply in the storage cistern if the mains water had to be shut off.

Cisterns

The 'tank' in your loft or attic is in fact a 'cistern'. Cisterns are not sealed – though they should be covered – and so are subject to atmospheric pressure. Tanks are completely sealed – as with a hot water storage tank – and are not subject to atmospheric pressure.

Cold water cisterns ,have traditionally been made of galvanised mild steel and it is quite likely that you will find one like this in your loft. They are still available, but are not usually installed in new houses. Other materials used have been asbestos, cement, copper and glass fibre, but today the most common material is plastic, of which glass fibre reinforced polyester (GRP), polythene and polypropylene are the most common varieties.

The advantages plastics have over all other cistern materials are their lightness in weight, resistance to corrosion and flexibility. Galvanised steel is heavy and liable to corrode, while asbestos and cement are not only heavy but can become porous and are prone to accidental damage. Don't forget the capacity of a typical cistern is 227 litres (50 gallons), and this water alone weighs nearly 0.25 tonne (¼ ton), so all cisterns must be fully supported on the joists. With rigid materials such as steel the cistern can rest across the joists, but with plastic and glass fibre a platform should be installed to support the whole area of the bottom, otherwise the material may develop local weaknesses.

Cisterns should be covered to prevent any contamination of the water. Where the underside of the roof is exposed dust and dirt are liable to fall in. The top and sides should also be insulated to minimise the risk of freezing. The bottom is left uncovered to allow rising warm air from rooms below to keep the water above freezing point, and so you shouldn't insulate the roof space under the cistern.

Cisterns were often installed before the roof was put on and if you want to replace yours, perhaps because it's made of steel and is corroding, you may not be able to get it through the trap door. While it is sometimes suggested that a cistern should be cut up to get it out this is in fact a very heavy and arduous job in such a confined space and it would be better to manoeuvre it to one side and leave it in the loft, installing a new cistern alongside. Modern plastic cisterns can literally be folded up so they can be passed through small loft hatches.

Pipes and taps

Water leaves the storage cistern in distribution pipes which are usually 22mm (¾in) or 15mm (½in) in diameter. In a direct system, supply from the cistern will usually only be to the hot water tank, and in an indirect system this link must also be direct – but other distribution pipes are used with branches to supply the other appliances – basins, baths and WC cisterns. Distribution pipes usually end in taps but in the case of a WC a low pressure ball-valve controls the flow.

The WC in an indirect system has a low pressure ball-valve because when the water leaves the storage cistern it is no longer at mains pressure but at normal atmospheric pressure which is pressing down on the surface of the stored water. This means that the higher up the house a tap or other outlet is situated the lower will be the water pressure. In practice this means that you can't have a tap in an indirect system which is above the level of its distribution outlet from the cistern. Showers are particularly affected by this difference of pressure, and if there is not sufficient 'head' to 'drive' the shower a special pump may have to be installed.

Cold water supplied to the hot water tank is heated in two different ways again called indirect and direct systems – or, respectively, closed and open. In the latter the cold water is circulated through the boiler, where it is heated, and returned to the tank from where it flows to tapped outlets. In the indirect system the cold water supplied never actually goes to the boiler, instead it is heated in the tank by a coiled pipe or jacket containing hot water which is continuously circulating through the boiler. In either case a pump often helps the water flow through the boiler, and supplementary or alternative heat may come from an immersion heater. If there is no boiler but only an immersion heater in the tank the system is essentially direct with the heating of the water taking place in the tank rather than in the boiler.

Draining the system

Just above the rising main stop-valve should be a drain cock. With the stop-valve turned off the drain cock can be used to drain part of the cold water system when repairs are necessary – the hot water system has its own drain cock.

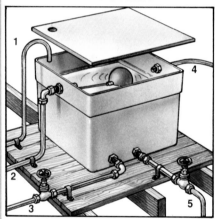

WASTE WATER SYSTEMS

A waste water system must be able to dispose of used water from the kitchen and bathroom efficiently and hygienically, and some also have to cater for rainwater falling on the roof. Here's how it's done.

The supply of hot and cold water to the taps in your house is really only half the domestic plumbing story. You also need a waste system to remove what you've used or don't want. And besides coping with the dirty water from the bath, basin and sink and the waste from the WC, the system also has to deal with the rainwater which falls on the roof.

The drainage system therefore has to be efficient and durable, and for obvious reasons of hygiene, self-cleansing. Waste matter mustn't be allowed to remain in the pipes and if blockages occur it should be possible to remove them easily.

How the drainage system works

There are several domestic drainage systems but each of them can be broken down into five separate sections. When waste water leaves an appliance of any sort, it will go immediately through a 'waste trap' – a 180° bend containing a water seal which fills the trap whenever the waste pipe empties. This keeps drain smells out of the room and prevents insects and the like from entering the home. With WCs it also makes self-cleansing easier. WC traps are cast as an integral part of the WC pan, but on other appliances they are separate, and are attached to the outlet pipe by a large retaining nut.

From the trap, waste water enters a branch pipe which leads to the main vertical drainage 'stack'. This takes it below ground level to the first underground section of the drainage system where it flows through at least one inspection chamber (covered with a manhole cover) and into the public sewer, which is usually situated underneath the road. The sewer is provided by the public health authority and it is their responsibility to remove all waste running into it.

Often rainwater from the roof is fed into the drainage system to flow into the public sewer. But some authorities provide a separate street drain for it or insist on the provision of soakaways (pits filled with rubble and gravel which allow the water to soak into the surrounding earth) near the house. Tanks and cisterns rarely overflow, but when they do they discharge clean water, so it's not necessary for the overflow pipes to be located over a drain.

The water can fall directly onto the ground.

The cost of laying public sewers in rural areas means that the waste from many houses in these parts flows into a cess pool or septic tank. These are specially constructed pits for storing effluent (and in the case of a septic tank, for breaking it down into harmless matter). Both of these require periodic pumping out, cess pools much more often as they store all the waste. If you're buying a house with one of these systems, check how often this has to be done, who does it and how much you may have to pay.

How it all began

Proper plumbing systems have only been around for about 100 years. The large urban expansion which took place during the Industrial Revolution lead to squalid housing conditions, and disease was rife. Eventually, enclosed sewers were introduced along with piped water supplies and pottery WC pans. By the 1870s many homes were equipped with a basin, a WC and a sink; but an acute shortage of qualified plumbers lead to ridiculous installations which often produced as great a health threat as before. The London County Council took the lead in sorting things out by laying out a set of rules in 1900, establishing the 'two-pipe' system – one stack for waste water from basins and sinks, another for 'soil water' from WCs.

The amount of pipework needed with the two-pipe system, and the increased siphonage problems on tall buildings, led to the introduction of the 'one-pipe' system. This system was the forerunner of the modern 'single stack' system and abandoned the distinction between the soil and the waste pipe stacks. It was only used extensively on multi-storey buildings.

On the one-pipe system all discharges flowed into a single stack which had an open-ended outlet at roof level. All traps had deep seals and each branch pipe was also connected to a vent pipe which rose to eaves level.

The single stack system was developed in the UK in the late 1940s to overcome the drawbacks and complications of the two-pipe systems, and to simplify the installation – everyone must be familiar with the untidy cluster of pipes on the outside walls of houses with these systems.

The advent of light plastic piping helped in this development, as it made the production of accurate mouldings easier, and cut down the installation time because plastic was quicker to join than the old metal piping.

The single stack system

This consists of a single waste stack into which all the branch pipes discharge. However, ground floor waste doesn't have to go

TWO-PIPE WASTE SYSTEM

The traditional two pipe system takes all soil to the underground drain by one pipe, and all the waste from baths, basins etc down another. It is found in most pre-war houses, and is still used, particularly in bungalows where the installation is spread out.

Roof drainage may flow into the same underground drainage system; it may go into a separate storm drain (out in the street) in areas of high rainfall; or it may drain into a soakaway in the garden.

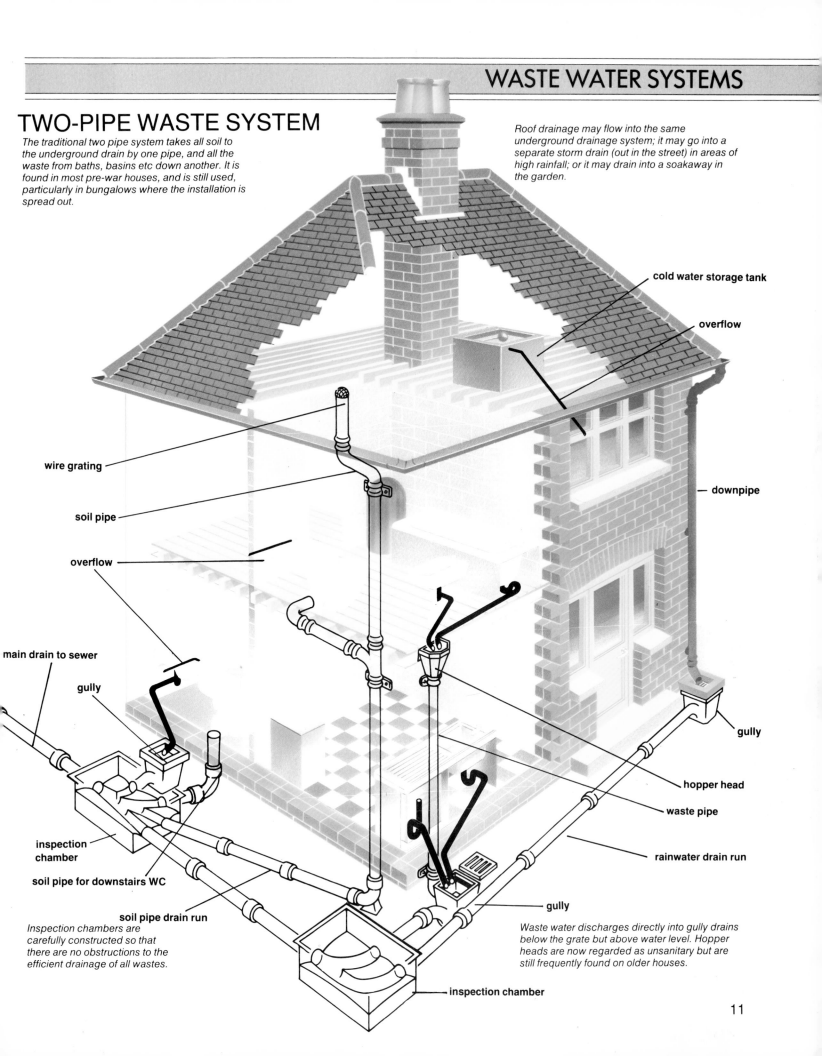

cold water storage tank

overflow

downpipe

wire grating

soil pipe

overflow

main drain to sewer

gully

gully

hopper head

waste pipe

rainwater drain run

inspection chamber

soil pipe for downstairs WC

soil pipe drain run

gully

Inspection chambers are carefully constructed so that there are no obstructions to the efficient drainage of all wastes.

Waste water discharges directly into gully drains below the grate but above water level. Hopper heads are now regarded as unsanitary but are still frequently found on older houses.

inspection chamber

11

SINGLE STACK WASTE SYSTEM

In most modern systems it is preferable to install a single stack system which involves less pipework provided that sources of waste are not too far from the stack itself.

In a single stack system the waste doesn't all have to go down the same stack – rainwater doesn't in any case. Ground floor waste and soil outlets can go direct into the underground drain. Waste outlets must discharge into trapped gullies. This arrangement is sometimes necessary where pipe runs get too long for the proper functioning of the single stack system or where the layout of appliances makes direct access to the drain more sensible.

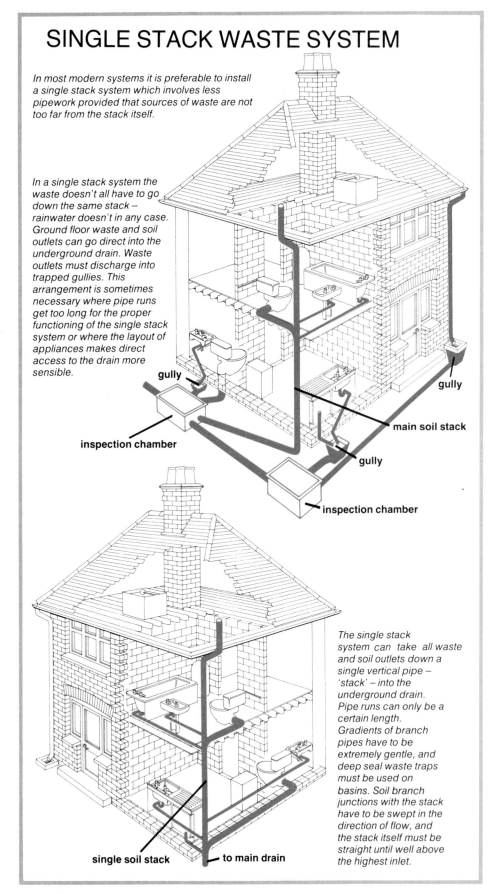

gully

inspection chamber

gully

main soil stack

gully

inspection chamber

The single stack system can take all waste and soil outlets down a single vertical pipe – 'stack' – into the underground drain. Pipe runs can only be a certain length. Gradients of branch pipes have to be extremely gentle, and deep seal waste traps must be used on basins. Soil branch junctions with the stack have to be swept in the direction of flow, and the stack itself must be straight until well above the highest inlet.

single soil stack   **to main drain**

into the stack. Sink waste water may flow into a trapped gully and ground-floor WCs may be connected directly into the underground drain. This avoids any risk that a blockage at the base of the stack (where it bends to join the underground drain) could lead to waste water being forced back along the waste pipes to ground-floor appliances.

In appearance the single-stack system is the simplest waste system of all and the most economical to install. As a result it is incorporated in the majority of new houses. But because the branches have to be comparatively short, the system is less useful in bungalows where appliances are likely to be spread out. Usually all the pipework is sited indoors, which means a neater appearance for the house exterior; it also reduces the possibility of frost damage. All you'll see of the system is a tell-tale vent pipe poking up through the roof.

In order to make the system work properly a number of technical regulations have to be taken into account when it's being installed. These relate to the length, diameter, bend radii and angles of bend of the branch pipes, the use of P-traps and S-traps on waste pipes other than WCs (see *Traps for each appliance*), the positioning of the stack connectors, and the dimensions of the stack itself. While the system may look simple, considerable research has been done to ensure that problems of siphonage aren't likely to occur.

The two-pipe system

The principles of the two-pipe system were based on a belief that all kinds of disease were caused by the 'bad air' in drains, and the system aimed to keep this out of homes. The basic principle was that the 'soil' discharge from WCs went directly down one stack into the underground drain. All other discharges, termed 'waste', went down another stack which led into a trapped gully (a cast drain incorporating a water trap) at ground level and from there joined the soil discharge under-ground. Sometimes waste had to fall into a channel at ground level before running into the drain.

All waste and soil pipework had to be fixed to the outside of the building. The soil pipe was continued upwards to eaves level where it terminated open-ended in a wire cover to keep nesting birds from causing a blockage. This allowed free passage of air from the underground drain.

When the two-pipe system came into existence, most homes only had an outside WC (quite often shared) and a kitchen sink, so discharge was entirely at ground level, but when upstairs bathrooms became popular waste was directed into hoppers attached to stand-pipes, which caused new problems. Hoppers were not self-cleansing and soapy water drying on the inside could start to smell; draughts could also blow up the pipe to the hopper, bringing smells from the drain at the bottom. This led to some authorities banning hoppers and insisting on discharge direct into another stack which meant installing an eaves-level vent as with the soil stack.

On buildings over two storeys high this created another problem known as 'induced siphonage'. When water flowing down the waste stack from one outlet passed another outlet where it joined the stack, it could cause a partial vacuum in the second pipe which could suck out the contents of the water trap. To cure this problem the upper part of each trap had to be connected to a branch vent pipe which either connected to a separate vertical stack to eaves level, or joined the vented waste stack at least 900mm (3ft) above the level of the highest waste connection. If you live in a tall house you may have this system, and any repairs to vent pipes should follow the existing system. The alternative is to take out the entire system and replace it with a single stack arrangement.

Traps for each appliance

The traditional trap was a simple U-shaped bend attached to a horizontal branch outlet – today called a 'P' trap. If the branch outlet is vertical this trap bends round again into a double 'U' or 'S' outlet. In systems with lead pipes, the traps were often formed from lengths of pipe, while with modern plastic waste systems the traps are separate and easily detachable. The plastic bottle trap, which performs the same function, is also now widely used, and this is more compact and neater in appearance.

The depth of the water-filled part of the trap is known as the 'depth of seal'. Shallow traps have a seal depth of around 50mm (2in), 38mm (1½in) or 19mm (¾in), while 'deep-seal' traps have a 75mm (3in) seal.

Lead traps usually allow access for clearing blockages, and this is obtained by unscrewing an access cap or 'eye'. Modern plastic traps are connected by screwed collars at both ends and can be completely removed for cleaning if blocked. The lower part of bottle traps likewise completely unscrews. Adjustable plastic traps are available for fixing to existing pipework where access is difficult and special adaptors are used to link to copper and iron pipes.

Traps must remain filled with water and it is against the bye-laws if they don't. This is the most important and lasting principle handed down from the waste disposal thinking of the last century.

The water seal can be lost from traps for lots of reasons. Siphonage is the worst problem and where it occurs it's usually due to a badly designed system. Simply, if the air pressure beyond the trap is slightly less than the normal atmospheric pressure acting on the surface of the water in the trap, the water will drain away. This is more likely with 'S' traps than 'P' traps, and with shallow rather than deep traps. The problem of siphonage led to the introduction of venting systems and dictated the dimensions in the single stack system (and also excluded the use of 'S' traps).

Overflow pipes

There are two sorts of overflow pipes – those which are connected to storage cisterns and WC cisterns, and those which are attached to or form a part of appliances such as basins and baths. They are known in the trade as warning pipes. Both sorts should be fitted to avoid the risk of overflows damaging your home. This may be caused when you forget to turn off the bath, or by mechanical failure when the ball-valve on the water storage tank jams open.

In sinks, basins and baths the overflow must discharge into the branch waste pipe between the trap and the appliance, or into the trap above the water level of the seal, and must be able to cope with the flow of water from one tap turned full on.

Sink and basin overflows are usually built into the design of the appliance, while those for baths are supplied as part of the plumbing and connect to a slot in the waste outlet casting.

Overflows from tanks and cisterns consist of a length of pipe of a minimum 22mm (⅞in) internal diameter, capable of discharging water as quickly as any incoming flow. They usually emerge through the outside wall and stick out far enough to avoid any water flow sluicing down the wall surface, which could be a potential source of damp.

Pipe and trap materials

All waste and soil pipes are today mainly manufactured in plastic. Branch pipes were made of lead or copper, stack pipes of cast iron, traps of lead or brass and underground pipes of vitrified clay. Only the latter still predominantly utilize the traditional material.

Your legal position

Drainage regulations fall under the Public Health Acts as well as the Building Regulations, so it's important to know where you stand. The householder is responsible for the entire drainage system until it enters the public sewer – even though this is usually beyond the boundary of the property. While blockages beyond the lowest inspection chamber are rare, any clearance work can be very expensive – particularly if you use a '24-hour' plumbing service. The public sewer is provided by the public health authority and is their responsibility.

If your house was built as one of a group of houses, then it's quite possible that you'll have shared drainage facilities. This means there is one drainage pipe collecting the waste of several homes before it discharges into the public sewer. The system was adopted because it saved installation costs. If your house was built before 1937, it's still the responsibility of the local authorities to cleanse the shared drainage runs, although you're responsible for clearing blockages and for maintenance. But if you live in a post-1937 house then the responsibility for the shared drains rests collectively on all the owners concerned and if a blockage is caused by someone else you will have to pay a proportion of the bill. It is therefore important when moving house to check out the exact position. If this is difficult to ascertain, try the Environmental Health Officer for advice; he should also be consulted if you want to change the system.

PLASTIC WASTE TRAPS

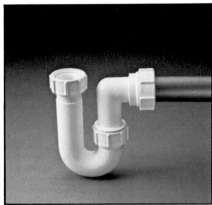

The modern U-bend is made from one of several plastic materials.

A U-bend with telescopic extension can be adjusted to existing appliances.

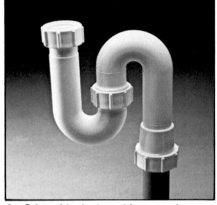

An S-bend is designed for use where the outlet is vertical.

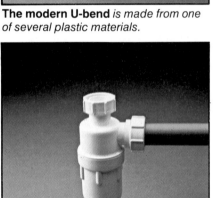

A bottle trap gives a neater appearance, but is less efficient.

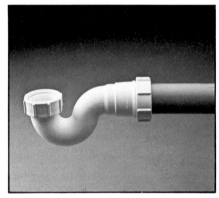

A shallow trap is used beneath a bath or shower where space is crucial.

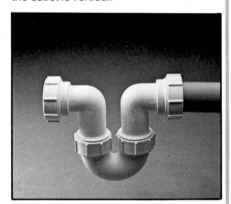

A running U-trap handles two or more untrapped appliances piped together.

A dip partition bottle trap has a base which unscrews.

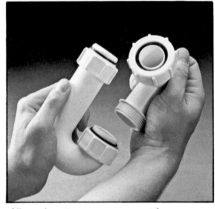

All modern traps come apart for easy cleaning and installation.

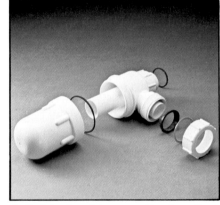

A dip tube trap taken apart to show the O rings and washers.

DRAINING PLUMBING SYSTEMS

When you are carrying out repairs or alterations to your plumbing or wet central heating system, you will usually have to drain water from the parts you are working on. Here's what you'll have to do.

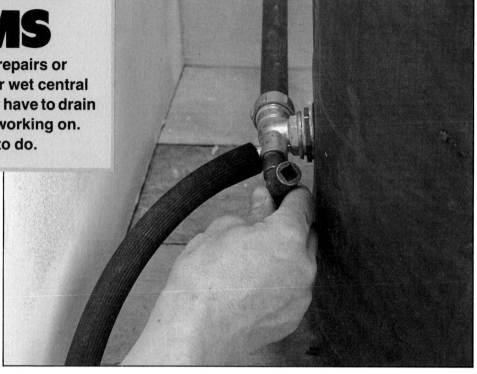

Virtually all major and many minor plumbing operations demand the partial or total drainage of either the domestic hot or cold water supply. If you have a 'wet' central heating system you'll also have to drain that before carrying out repairs or alterations. Before attempting this – long before the need for drainage arises, in fact – you should make yourself thoroughly familiar with the design and layout of these systems in your home. Here are some questions to which you should know the answers:

● Are all cold water draw-off points supplied direct from the rising main, or are the bathroom cold taps and the WC cistern supplied with water from a main cold water storage cistern (probably situated in the roof space)?

● Is the hot water system 'direct' or 'indirect' (see pages 9 to 13)?

● If the system is direct, is the domestic hot water heated solely by means of an electric immersion heater, solely by means of a domestic boiler (gas, oil or solid fuel), or are both means of heating available?

● If hot water is provided solely by means of an immersion heater, is there a drain-valve at the base of the cold supply pipe from the storage cistern to the hot water cylinder?

● If hot water is provided by means of a boiler, is there a drain-valve on the pipework beside the boiler, or possibly incorporated into the boiler itself?

● If the system is indirect, is it a conventional indirect system (indicated by the presence of a small feed-and-expansion tank in the roof space, feeding the primary circuit) or is it a self-priming indirect system such as the Primatic?

● Is there a 'wet' central heating system provided in conjunction with hot water supply?

● Where is the main stop-valve, and are there any other stop-valves or gate-valves fitted into distribution or circulating pipes in the system?

● Are there drain-valves at low points in the central heating circuit?

Draining down for simple repairs

Once you are thoroughly familiar with the contents and layout of your own plumbing and central heating systems, you will be able to work out for yourself how much draining-down will be necessary before you undertake any particular item of maintenance or any particular project. If, for instance, you wish to rewasher the cold tap over the kitchen sink (this is supplied direct from the rising main) or to tee into the rising main to provide a garden water supply, all that you need to do is to turn off the main stop-valve and to turn on the kitchen cold tap until water ceases to flow from it. You will then have drained the rising main to the level of the cold tap. In many modern homes a drain-valve is provided immediately above the main stop-valve to permit the rising main to be completely drained.

Rather more drainage is necessary when you wish to renew the washer on a hot tap, or on a cold tap supplied from a storage cistern, or to renew a ball-valve in a WC cistern that is supplied with water from a storage cistern. First of all, see if there are any stop-valves or gate-valves on the distribution pipes leading to the particular tap or ball-valve. There could be gate-valves on the main hot and cold distribution pipes just below the level of the main cold water storage cistern. There could even be a mini-stop-valve on the distribution pipe immediately before its connection to the tail of the tap or ball-valve.

In either of these circumstances you're in luck! All you have to do is to turn off the appropriate gate-valve or mini-stop-valve and then to turn on the tap or flush the lavatory cistern. You can then carry out the necessary repairs.

Avoiding unnecessary drainage

The chances are, though, that the main stop-valve will be the only one in the system, and that you'll have to contemplate draining the main cold water storage cistern and the appropriate distribution pipes before you can get on with your task, by turning off the main stop-valve and draining the cistern and pipes from the taps supplied by the cistern. This, however, will mean that the whole of the plumbing system is out of action for as long as it takes you to complete the job. It is generally better to go up into the roof space and lay a slat of wood across the top of the cold water storage cistern. You can then tie the float arm of the ball-valve up to it, so that water cannot flow into the cistern. Then drain the cistern by opening the bathroom taps. In this way the cold tap over the sink will not be put out of action.

Here's another useful money-saving tip: even if you are draining down to rewasher a hot tap, there is no need to run to waste all that hot water stored in the hot water cylinder, *provided that your bathroom cold taps are supplied from the cold water storage cistern*. Having tied up the ball-valve, run the bathroom *cold* taps until they cease to flow and only then turn on the hot tap you want to work on. Because the hot water distribution pipe is taken from above the hot water storage cylinder, only a little hot water – from the pipe itself – will flow away to waste and the cylinder will remain full of hot water.

For the same reason, unless you expect to have the hot water system out of action for a

WHERE TO DRAIN THE SYSTEM

On a well-designed plumbing system you should find that drain-valves have been installed at several points, so that partial draining-down is possible.

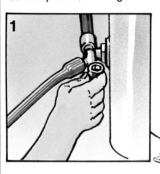

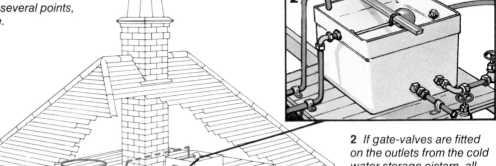

1 A drain-valve at the point where the cold feed from the storage cistern in the loft enters the hot water cylinder means that you can empty the main body of the cylinder (at least, down to the level of the inlet pipe) in the event of it springing a leak. Here a T-shaped drain-valve spanner is being used to open the valve.

3 Drain-valves fitted beside the boiler allow you to drain the primary circuit and the central heating system.

2 If gate-valves are fitted on the outlets from the cold water storage cistern, all you have to do to drain a pipe run is shut the appropriate valve and open the taps. If they are not fitted, you will have to drain the cistern too. To stop it filling, tie the float arm up to a piece of wood resting across the cistern.

4 A drain-valve fitted above the rising main stop-valve allows you to drain the main and connect tees to it. The stop-valve saves you from having to tie up the storage cistern ball-valve when draining the cold supply pipes.

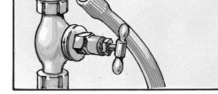

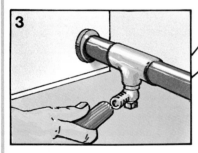

Action checklist
Which part of the system you drain, and how you go about it, depends on the job you're doing. Here's a brief checklist of the sequence of operations in each case.

Job: *to rewasher/replace kitchen cold tap, tee off rising main for new supply pipe;*
● *turn off rising main stop-valve and drain rising main via drain-valve*
● *if no drain-valve fitted, open kitchen cold tap to drain main down to level of tee to kitchen sink.*

Job: *to rewasher/replace other cold tap, renew WC ball-valve, extend cold supply;*
● *if gate-valve fitted to outlet at cold cistern, close valve and open lowest appropriate cold tap; otherwise*
● *tie up arm of cold cistern ball-valve and drain cistern by opening cold taps.*

Job: *to rewasher/replace hot tap, extend existing hot supply;*
● *close gate-valve on outlet at cistern or tie up cistern ball-valve*
● *open cold tap until flow stops*
● *only then open hot tap.*

Job: *to replace hot cylinder;*
● *close gate-valve or tie up ball-valve arm*
● *turn off boiler or immersion heater*
● *empty cylinder via cylinder drain-valve*
● *close gate-valve on outlet from feed/ expansion tank, or tie up ball-valve*
● *drain primary circuit via drain-valve at boiler.*

Job: *to replace cold cistern;*
● *close rising main stop-valve*
● *drain cistern by opening cold taps (hot water will still run from cylinder).*

Job: *to replace boiler;*
● *on direct systems, turn off boiler or immersion heater and also heating system*
● *close rising main stop-valve*
● *open all taps, and drain boiler from drain-valve nearby*
● *on indirect systems, turn off boiler*
● *close feed/expansion tank gate-valve*
● *drain primary and central heating systems from drain-valves at boiler.*

prolonged period there is no need to switch off the immersion heater or to let out the boiler when carrying out a maintenance operation on the bathroom hot tap.

Problems with air locks
If your hot and cold water distribution systems are properly designed – with 'horizontal' runs of pipe actually having a slight fall away from the storage cistern or the vent pipe to permit air to escape – then the system should fill up with little or no trouble when you untie the ball-valve and permit water to flow into the cistern again. Should an air-lock prevent complete filling, try connecting one end of a length of hose to the cold tap over the kitchen sink and the other end to one of the taps giving trouble. Turn on first the tap giving trouble and then the one over the kitchen sink. Mains pressure from this cold tap should blow the air bubble out of the system.

Draining the whole system
Very occasionally – perhaps because of a major reconstruction of the system or because of that most traumatic of all plumbing emergencies, a leaking boiler – it may be necessary to drain the whole system. Let's assume, first of all, that you have either a direct hot water system or a self-priming indirect one.

Switch off the immersion heater and let out or switch off the boiler. Turn off the central heating system if this is operated from the self-priming cylinder. Close the main stop-valve and open up every tap in the house – hot as well as cold. Connect one end of a length of hose to the drain-valve beside the boiler or, if the cylinder is heated by an immersion heater only, at the base of the cold supply pipe entering the cylinder, and take the other end of the hose to an outside gully. Open up the drain-valve and allow the system to drain.

If you have an indirect system you should again turn off the boiler and central heating system. Then close the gate-valve leading from the feed-and-expansion tank, or tie up it's ball-valve, and drain the system from the boiler drain-valves.

How you proceed depends upon the reason for which you have carried out the draining-down. Your aim should be to get as much of the plumbing system as possible back into operation quickly.

Restoring partial supplies
The first step is to go up into the roof space and tie up the ball-valve on the main storage cistern as already described. Open up the main stop-valve and water supply will be restored to the cold tap over the kitchen sink.

It should also be possible to restore the bathroom cold water supplies. Trace the distribution pipe that takes water from the cold water storage cistern to the hot water cylinder.

COPING WITH AIRLOCKS
Clear supply-pipe airlocks by linking the affected tap to the kitchen cold tap with hose secured by worm-drive clips. Open the affected tap first, then the kitchen tap.

Avoid airlocks in primary or heating circuits by filling them upwards via a hose linking the kitchen cold tap and the boiler drain-valve. Close vents as radiators fill.

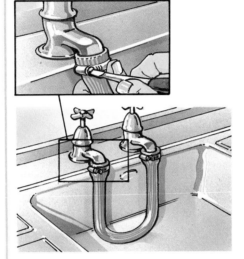
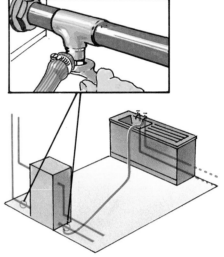

Find a cork of the correct size, lean into the cistern and push it into the pipe's inlet. Before doing so, it is a good idea to screw a substantial woodscrew part of the way into the cork to facilitate removal. You can then untie the ball-valve and allow the cistern to refill; no water will flow to the hot cylinder.

Draining heating systems
If you have a conventional indirect hot water system – perhaps installed in conjunction with a central heating system – you can drain the primary circuit, together with the radiator circuit if there is one, without draining the water from the outer part of the storage cylinder. Because of the increased risk of corrosion that arises from water and air coming into contact with steel surfaces, a radiator circuit should be drained only when absolutely essential. When this has to be done – to add additional radiators, perhaps – you should tie up the ball-valve serving the feed-and-expansion tank and drain from both the drain-valve beside the boiler and from any drain-valves provided at low points of the system. You must, of course, let out or switch off the boiler before attempting this.

When refilling the primary circuit (or when refilling a direct system with boiler) it may help to prevent the formation of air-locks if you connect one end of your garden hose to the boiler drain-valve and the other end to the cold tap over the kitchen sink. Open them both up and the system will fill upwards, with air being driven out in front of the rising water. As the central heating circuit refills,

open up all the radiator vents – and any other air vents that there may be in the system – and leave them open until water begins to flow through them. It is a good idea, when refilling a central heating system, to introduce a reliable corrosion-proofer into the feed-and-expansion tank to prevent future internal corrosion, but you can do this only if you fill the system from the top, not from the bottom.

Winter precautions
One final point: if you are leaving your home empty during the winter months, you should drain the main cold water storage cistern and, if you have a direct hot water system and will be away for more than two or three days, you should drain the hot cylinder, the boiler and its circulation pipes as well. Human memory is fallible. Having done so, leave a conspicuous notice on the boiler and by the immersion heater switch saying 'SYSTEM DRAINED – DO NOT LIGHT BOILER OR SWITCH ON HEATER UNTIL IT HAS BEEN REFILLED'.

Because of the risk of corrosion already referred to, the primary circuit and any central heating system connected to it should not be drained in these circumstances. If you have a central heating system that is capable of automatic control, leave it switched on under the control of a frost-stat. This is a thermostatic control, usually positioned in a garage or in the roof space, that will bring the heating into operation when a predetermined, near-freezing-point temperature, is reached.

INSTALLING A SINK UNIT

The sink is a highly important item of kitchen equipment, and replacing an old model is usually one of the first priorities for anyone modernising their kitchen. In this article we consider the range available and how to fit them.

If your house was built in the 1930s or 1940s, and the kitchen has never been modernised, the chances are that it contains the original deep white glazed stoneware 'Belfast pattern' sink, supported by heavy cast-iron brackets built into the wall. It will incorporate a weir overflow and will probably have a detachable wooden draining board. A deep sink of this kind was regarded as the height of domestic luxury in the pre-war and early post-war years. An even older property might have a shallow yellow 'London pattern' sink, probably supported by brick pillars. In either case the water will very likely come from brass bib-taps (taps with horizontal inlets) projecting from a tiled splash-back fixed to the wall behind the sink. Old London pattern sinks were sometimes installed with an untrapped waste that passed through the kitchen wall to discharge over an outside gully drain. More recent sinks would have a lead or brass U-trap screwed to the waste outlet from which a branch waste pipe would discharge over the gully.

Sink units
Because these old stoneware sinks were certain death to crockery dropped into them, and looked increasingly dated, they were gradually replaced by sink units with one-piece sink tops. The sink tops were made of enamelled pressed steel or stainless steel, and the units into which they were fixed became the starting point for complete kitchen ranges incorporating continuous work surfaces. The early enamelled pressed steel sink tops had the disadvantage that the enamel was vulnerable to accidental damage. Dropping any hard object onto them could easily chip or crack the enamel. The stainless steel sink therefore became the most important innovation.

Taps and traps
It was usual, when replacing an old stoneware sink with a stainless steel or an enamelled pressed-steel sink, to get rid of the old bib-taps projecting from the wall, and to replace them with chromium-plated brass pillar taps or a mixer fitted into the

holes provided at the back of the sink and connected to the hot and cold water distribution pipes concealed within the unit.

Early sinks of this kind were provided with traps, also concealed within the unit. The trap might still be of brass with a copper waste pipe, but plastic was soon introduced, connected to a plastic waste pipe by means of ring-seal push-fit connectors. Bottle traps, as distinct from the traditional U-traps, became increasingly popular. They were neater in appearance, space saving and easy to dismantle in case of a blockage, although their discharge rate was not as great. Modern ground floor sinks often still discharge over a yard gully, but the waste pipe outlet should be taken to below the gully grid either through a slotted grid or by the use of a back or side-inlet gully.

Overflows
Early sink tops had a built-in overflow consisting of a unit welded to the back of the sink. But these inevitably leaked after a time, and nowadays they have been replaced by a flexible overflow pipe. This is like the overflow pipe from a bath which is taken from the sink's overflow outlet to connect, by means of a sleeve or 'banjo' fitting, to the slotted waste pipe, before its connection to the trap. Householders who possess a sink of the older pattern with a leaking built-in overflow, will find that if the sink is dismounted and turned upside down, the overflow unit can be sawn off and replaced with one of the more modern waste and overflow fittings. But, of course, it may be better to replace the the sink.

New developments
Nowadays, there is no question of being restricted to a single sink with either right or left-hand drainer. Double sinks, one for washing the crockery and cutlery and the other for a hot rinse before air drying, have become more and more popular. The two sinks may be of equal size, around 450mm (18in) in width, or one may be smaller than the other for use in food preparation. A second sink like this might be only 240mm (10in) in width. There are also sinks with double drainers, though these are rather less in demand as they take up a lot of space; they are usually around 2m (6ft 6in) long. Overall sizes of rectangular sinks and drainer units range from about 900mm (3ft) to 1500mm (5ft) in length, and usually measure 500 or 600mm (20 to 24in) deep, to fit metric base units. Some sink tops are still available in the 21in (533mm) size to match old imperial base units. There are also many intermediate sizes, and bowl depths may range between 130 and 180mm (5 and 7in).

Early glass-reinforced plastic sink tops and drainers proved to be a complete disaster. They were incapable of standing up to the very heavy use to which sinks are subjected, their colours faded and they cracked, and crazed. Considerable advances have since been made, and modern plastic sinks and sink tops seem well able to stand up to everything that is required of them.

Ceramic sinks are making a come back, though they are very different from the old Belfast and London pattern sinks. Modern ranges include tough inset sinks and tops in an attractive range of colours. There are inset round bowls 450mm (18in) in diameter with an accompanying but separate round drainer 380mm (15in) in diameter. Then there is a conventional rectangular double sink and drainer – all of ceramic ware – in an overall size of 1125 x 505mm (45 x 20in). There is also a conventional rectangular single sink and drainer and round double sinks and drainer in one unit. A feature of these new ceramic units is their extreme toughness.

The waste and overflow of the new ceramic sinks are arranged in exactly the same way as those of the old Belfast models. A built-in overflow connects to the slot in a slotted waste outlet that is bedded on mastic in the outlet hole. Stainless steel sinks are provided with the flexible overflow already referred to, which connects to the slotted waste below the sink but above the trap. Double sinks have only one trap. This is fitted into the outlet of the sink nearest to the drain outlet, the waste from the other sink being connected to it above the level of the single trap.

Mixers

Individual sink pillar taps are still freely available, but the choice nowadays is more likely to be a sink mixer. A mixer with a swivel spout is an essential where a double sink is installed.

Sink mixers differ from bath and basin mixers in one important respect. The latter are simply two taps with a single spout. The hot and cold streams of water mix within the body of the mixer unit. Sink mixers have

separate channels for the hot and cold streams of water which mix in the air as they leave the spout. The reason for this is that the cold water supply to the kitchen sink (the household's supply of water for drinking and cooking) comes direct from the rising main. The hot supply usually comes from a cylinder storage hot water system, fed with water from a main cold water storage cistern. It is illegal to mix, in one fitting, water from the main and water from a storage cistern.

Everybody is familiar with the conventional sink mixer, made of chromium-plated brass with 'shrouded' cross-top handles of plastic and a long swivel spout. Nowadays, though, there are some exciting new designs available. With some the mixer unit is fitted into just one hole at the back of the sink. The other hole may be blanked off or may be used to accommodate a rinsing brush, supplied with hot water by a flexible tube connected to the hot water supply pipe.

Putting in the sink top

When you come to install your new sink it's a good idea to make the first job fitting the taps or mixer, waste and overflow to it. This will avoid unnecessary interruption to the rest of the plumbing services. Start by putting in the combined waste and overflow unit, then attach the taps or mixer. If the sink is made of stainless steel the shanks of the taps will protrude through the holes so you won't be able to screw up the back-nuts tight. Use 'top hat' washers or spacers to accommodate the shanks.

When the sink is in position the tap tails will usually be fairly inaccessible, so it may be a

good idea to attach purpose-made extension pieces to bring them to a level below the sink basin where they will be accessible.

When you've got the new sink top ready, you'll have to turn off the main stop-valve and drain the hot and cold water pipes which supply the existing sink. Then you can disconnect the waste outlet, and use a cold chisel and hammer to chip away any seal between the back of the sink and the wall. You can remove the old sink (remember, it's going to be very heavy) and saw off the heavy cantilevered brackets that supported the old sink flush with the wall.

The hot and cold water supply pipes to the bib-taps over the old sink will probably be chased (inset) into the wall, so you'll have to unscrew and remove the old taps, excavate the pipes from the wall and pull them forward so that they can be connected to the tails of new taps.

With the new sink unit in position, the next job is to cut the water supply pipes to the correct length to connect to the tails of the taps. The sink top simply rests on the sink unit, so the tails of the taps can now be connected to the water supply pipes. If the trap of the old sink will connect to the new waste it can be reused.

THE PLUMBING CONNECTIONS

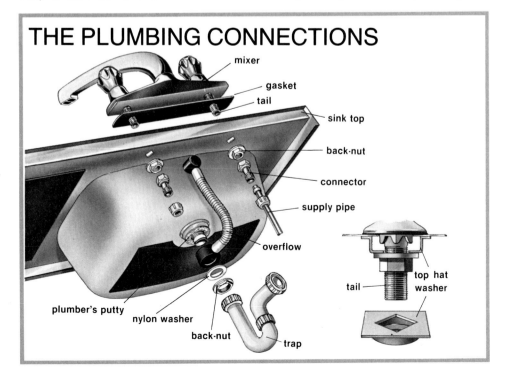

INSTALLING A SINK TOP

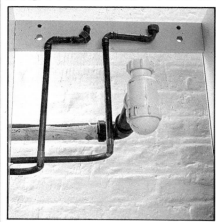

1 Take out your old sink top and check that the existing plumbing connections are undamaged. Replace as necessary.

2 Place your new sink top downwards on the floor. Take the waste outlet and press plumber's putty around the top of the screw.

3 Press the outlet firmly into position in the sink outlet aperture, at the same time squeezing out excess putty. Then put on the plastic washer.

6 Place the outlet collar of the banjo unit firmly on top of the plastic washer and support it with one hand before putting on the back-nut.

7 Put on the back-nut and screw it up tightly against the banjo unit collar, making sure it runs straight towards the sink outlet hole.

8 Screw up the overflow rose to the banjo unit overflow pipe. To help get it tight, hold the back of the outlet with a pair of pliers.

11 Take the mixer unit and ensure that the rubber gasket has no grit on it; then place the inlet tails into the holes and press the unit into position.

12 Screw on the inlet tail back-nuts and tighten them, making sure the gasket remains flat. You don't need to use any plumber's putty.

13 When the outlet and mixer installation is complete, lift the sink top into its correct position and screw it to the kitchen unit.

4 With the plastic washer pushed firmly home, take a roll of PTFE tape and run it around the thread right up to the end of the outlet.

5 Before putting on the banjo unit run a thick film of pipe-jointing compound around the uppermost surface of the plastic washer.

9 Run a knife around the edge of the plumber's putty squeezed out from around the outlet flange. Be careful not to score the metal.

10 Peel away the surplus putty and check that the outlet flange is tightly held into the sink. If not, tighten the back-nut further.

14 Attach the inlet pipes to the mixer tails and tighten the nuts with a crowsfoot spanner, which helps you reach them.

15 Check that the old trap is clear and screw it up tightly to the outlet pipe; then turn on the taps to check that there are no leaks.

Ready Reference

SINK DESIGNS

Sink designs come in several different variations particularly in the inset range. Think carefully about what you use your sink for, and what space you have available before deciding on size and design.

TYPICAL SINK SIZES

S=single, D=double, Si=sink, Dr=drainer

	Tops	Inset
SDrSSi	42x31in	37x19in
	1000x500mm	940x485mm
	1000x600mm	
	1200x600mm	
DDrSSi	63x21in	55x19in
	1500x500mm	1395x485mm
	1500x600mm	
SDrDSi	63x21in	55x19in
	1500x600mm	1395x485mm
DDrDSi	84x21in	74x19in
	2000x600mm	1850x485mm

TYPICAL DESIGNS

If you don't have a dishwasher a double bowl is useful – one for washing and one for rinsing.

double bowl

A double drainer will give you a greater working area at the sink but will cut down on the remainder of your work surface.

double drainer

If you're short of space you may dispense with the drainer altogether and use an inset bowl only. There are also units with small subsidiary bowls specially incorporated to house a waste disposal unit. These may also be supplied with trays which fit in or over the bowl, facilitating such tasks as salad preparation.

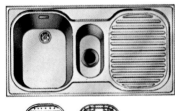

disposal sink and trays

21

INSTALLING AN INSET SINK

If you're fitting a new kitchen, or modernising an old one, one job you'll almost certainly have to carry out is to install an inset sink into a worktop.

Not so long ago, an assortment of cupboards, work surfaces and a kitchen sink unit formed the framework of the average kitchen. It was not a particularly efficient arrangement, but because few appliances had to be fitted in it didn't matter too much if a little space was wasted. However, as more and more homes acquired washing machines, tumble dryers, refrigerators and the like, some way had to be found of fitting these appliances into what was often a relatively small area.

What resulted from this was the 'integral' kitchen which housed all this equipment under roomy and well-lit worktops. And hand in hand with this development went the introduction of the inset sink.

The old enamelled and stainless steel sit-on sinks, with their single or double drainers, completely covered their base units. From a functional point of view they were ideal because the one-piece top meant that it was virtually impossible for water to seep into the cupboard below. Yet the kitchen sink remained a conspicuous, and somewhat unattractive, feature, divorced from other kitchen surfaces. And because of the space it took up, the unit was restricted to only one or two positions in the room. Consequently, many kitchens had to be planned around it, which naturally limited the ways in which they could be made more labour-saving and pleasant to work in.

However, once the move to creating uninterrupted work surfaces took hold, the benefits of installing a 'built-into-the-worktop' sink became readily apparent. For the first time it meant that a sink could be fitted into an overall design, which could still retain a clean, streamlined look. It didn't have to be fitted directly over a base unit, which gave far more flexibility as to where it could be positioned. However, there still had to be sufficient clearance under the worktop to take the bowl, and the plumbing supply and waste runs still had to make sense.

In fact, the idea for inset sinks stemmed from bathroom and bedroom vanity units, where a washbasin was let into the surface of a small cupboard. The surrounding melamine-finished surface was easy to clean and provided a standing area for bottles, cosmetics and the like. It was only a matter of time before the idea was adopted in the kitchen.

Choosing an inset sink

Whether you're revamping your kitchen, or just modernising the existing sink, there are a number of points to take into account before buying a new inset model.

The first is to decide what exactly the sink has to handle, because this will give you a fair guide as to the size you'll need, and whether two bowls would be better instead of just one. Indeed, there are a number of advantages in installing two or even two-and-a-half bowls (the 'half' being specifically for cutlery) not the least being that you'll still have access to the taps even if one bowl is occupied. And the amount of extra plumbing you'll have to carry out is quite small. All it entails is slightly extending the waste run. If you install a mixer tap with a swivel spout this can be used to fill both bowls so there's no additional work on the water supply side.

As with sit-on sinks, there is a wide range of bowl/drainer combinations. There are also individual round bowls which don't have an attached drainer, although there are separate drainers available that you have to let into the worktop nearby.

Round bowls do look attractive and they are increasing in popularity, but they have a couple of disadvantages. They tend to be shallower than the traditional rectangular shape – generally, the deeper the bowl the better – and their shape sometimes makes it awkward to submerge large pans and grill trays when they're being washed.

Which material to go for?

The other main consideration when choosing a sink is the material it's made of. Nowadays there is a far wider choice than ever before.

Stainless steel has retained its popularity, principally because it is relatively cheap and there is a wide range of styles available. Yet while it is heat-resistant and hard wearing, it can suffer at the hands of scourers and abrasive cleaners which leave minute surface scratches. You may also find this material somewhat clinical in appearance. However, if you do there are alternatives.

Don't shy away from plastic, for example. Admittedly the early glass-reinforced plastic tops proved to be a disaster: they simply weren't sturdy enough to cope with the use – and misuse – a kitchen sink is subjected to. But the ones on sale now are vastly different. These are made of impact-resistant modified polycarbonate in a range of attractive colours that extend right through the material. You can buy double as well as single sinks with round or rectangular bowls. As far as temperature resistance is concerned these sinks are very tough, and to prove it they are put through some remarkably nasty tests. One manufacturer, for example, has tested such sinks in hot water at up to 95°C for 40 days, in boiling water at five different levels of water hardness for 50 hours and by placing hot

THE PLUMBING CONNECTIONS

Right: Each bowl outlet should be connected to a 75mm (3in) deep seal P- or S-trap which is linked to 38mm (1 1/2in) UPVC waste pipe. The overflows should connect to the outlets above the traps. You may have to move the supply pipes away from the wall so they can reach the tap positions.

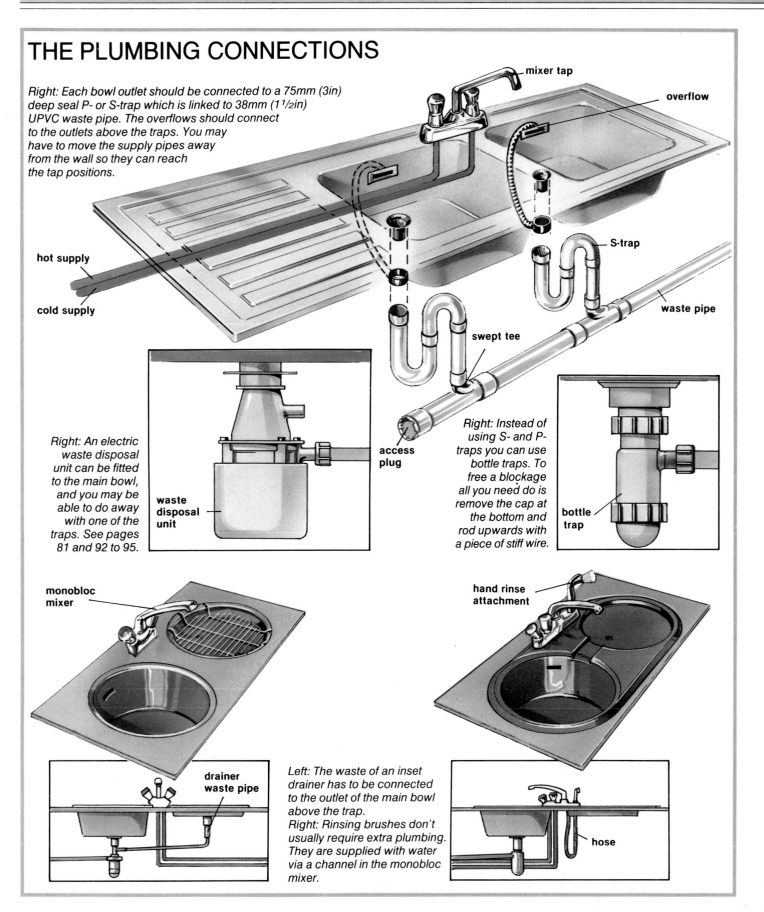

mixer tap

overflow

hot supply

cold supply

S-trap

waste pipe

swept tee

access plug

waste disposal unit

bottle trap

monobloc mixer

hand rinse attachment

drainer waste pipe

hose

Right: An electric waste disposal unit can be fitted to the main bowl, and you may be able to do away with one of the traps. See pages 81 and 92 to 95.

Right: Instead of using S- and P- traps you can use bottle traps. To free a blockage all you need do is remove the cap at the bottom and rod upwards with a piece of stiff wire.

Left: The waste of an inset drainer has to be connected to the outlet of the main bowl above the trap.
Right: Rinsing brushes don't usually require extra plumbing. They are supplied with water via a channel in the monobloc mixer.

INSTALLING AN INSET SINK

1 If space is limited and the worktop is fixed in position, check underneath that there is clearance for the bowls and then mark round the template.

2 Drill a hole through the worktop on the waste side of the cut-out. Insert the jigsaw and cut out the hole, supporting the waste on the underside.

3 Test fit the sink in the hole, wriggling it a little to get it to drop down flush with the top. If it sticks, file back the area where it catches.

6 If the sink doesn't have a tap hole punched, place the special template over the knockout and gently use a hammer and punch to make one.

7 Insert the monobloc mixer, making sure that it sits on a rubber gasket. Then use a spanner to tighten the back-nut underneath the sink.

8 Make up the outlets for the main and half bowls and the overflow. Some outlets are bedded on plumber's putty while others sit on special plastic washers.

saucepans on them for short periods at temperatures up to 180°C. No domestic sink is likely to experience anything like that amount of misuse; even so the sinks weathered the punishment.

Ceramic sinks are once more on the market and are becoming increasingly popular. Again, they are very different from their early counterparts, but one thing hasn't changed. They spell certain death to any piece of crockery dropped into them. It's a point that should perhaps be borne in mind when choosing a sink top. Having said this, these sinks are available in an attractive range of colours (you can even get a mixer tap to match), and as with plastic and stainless steel models some versions have integral drainers. Once installed these sinks are highly resistant to being damaged. However, if you do plump for a ceramic sink and you want to install a waste disposal unit check

that the two are compatible, because it's impossible to widen the outlet as you can do with a stainless steel top.

Choosing the taps
Apart from all the other considerations it's important to choose an inset sink with the taps in mind.

If you go for a two or two-and-a-half bowl top then you're going to need some form of swivel mixer. Some sinks will only take a monobloc mixer because there is only one access hole for the hot and cold supply pipes. Others take conventional mixers. Alternatively, you could use separate pillar taps.

Some sink tops are reversible, in that depending on which way round you fit them they can have a left-hand or right-hand drainer. Obviously you can't have tap holes on both sides of the bowl, so to get round the problem usually there are knockouts in the

potential tap sites and you just remove those you want to use.

Sometimes no provision is made for taps. In this case you'll have to install bib taps coming out of the wall or drill holes through the worktop itself and fit the taps to these.

How to install an inset sink
Installing an inset sink presents no special difficulties. As with conventional sinks, and indeed most other plumbing fittings, it's best to carry out as much work as possible before putting the worktop in position. But if the worktop is fixed, rather than remove it work in situ instead. First, fit the taps. With a mixer you'll need a flat washer between the base and the sink top. And for a plastic or stainless steel sink, you'll probably need to use top hat or spacer washers over the tap tails to accommodate the protruding shanks before screwing on the back-nuts.

4 *Some sinks are bedded on a rubber or plastic seal. If not, run silicone rubber or non-setting mastic round the edge of the hole before fitting the sink.*

5 *Lower the inset sink into the hole and then fasten it in position underneath using the clips provided. Clean away any sealant that oozes from the edges.*

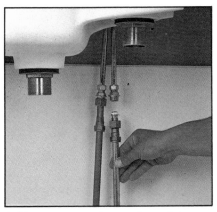

9 *Use tap connectors and special reducers to connect the 15mm (1/2in) hot and cold supply runs to the tap tails, which on this model are slightly narrower.*

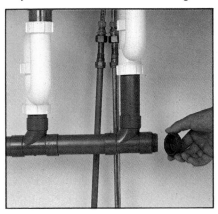

10 *Use S-traps and swept tees to connect the 38mm (1 1/2in) wastes to a common waste run. An inspection eye at the end of the run aids blockage removal.*

The tap tails will be difficult to get to once the sink is in position, particularly if the unit you are fitting over has a back to it. Therefore it's best to fit a small run of pipe, or lengths of corrugated flexible pipe, to each of the tap tails at this stage.

The waste and overflow unit is usually supplied with the sink. Don't forget to bed the outlet on a layer of mastic, and as you tighten up the back-nut make sure the slot in the shank points in the direction of the overflow. Next, screw the overflow to the outlet point at the top of the sink bowl and then slip the 'banjo' connector at the other end of the flexible hose over the slotted waste. This is held in place by another back-nut.

As far as marking out the work surface is concerned, most sink manufacturers supply a template indicating the area of worktop to be removed. Needless to say this must be done with care and accuracy, and for this reason it's best to work on the top surface and not the underside so there's no risk of getting the sink in the wrong place.

Drill a hole through the waste side of the cut-out and then use a jigsaw to cut the hole. You can then fit the retaining brackets or rim round the underside edge. The fixing clips on the sink are secured to these when it's set in its final position.

Usually, inset sinks are provided with a rubber seal or gasket so that when fitted there's a watertight seal between the bowl and drainer and the worktop. If there isn't one, run a continuous bead of non-setting mastic round the perimeter and bed the top firmly onto this.

Once you've lowered the sink into position and clipped it in place all that then remains is to set the worktop in position on top of the unit and to connect the waste pipe and the hot and cold supply runs.

Ready Reference

CHECK UNDERSURFACE CLEARANCE

You've got considerable flexibility as to where you position an inset sink – it need not necessarily be directly over a base unit. But wherever you propose to site it make sure there is sufficient depth under the worktop to accommodate the bowls.

WHICH SINK TO CHOOSE

Inset sinks can have one, two or two and a half bowls. Some incorporate drainers, but with individual bowls separate drainers have to be installed alongside.

Many inset sinks are made of stainless steel, but if you choose a plastic or ceramic sink you have the added option of a wide range of colours.

TIP: CARE WITH HOT PANS

Whatever material your sink is made of it will withstand all likely treatment. If you've a plastic sink it's advisable not to put frying pans that have just been used for frying hot meat, dry cooked foods and hot oil directly in the sink. First allow the pan to cool briefly.

TIP: FITTING A WASTE DISPOSER

If you're installing a ceramic sink and you also want a waste disposal unit, make sure the outlet of the sink is compatible with the inlet on the disposer. Ceramic sinks can't be cut, so the two must match exactly.

BOWL ACCESSORIES

There are various accessories you can fit over the bowl of the sink such as a draining tray (A) and a chopping board (B). Ideally, use the chopping board over the sink with a waste disposer so that any vegetable matter can be hygienically flushed away.

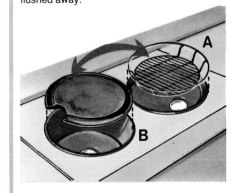

PLUMBING IN KITCHEN APPLIANCES

Washing machines and dishwashers can be a great boon in the house. They are best plumbed into a water supply and the waste outlet, otherwise you'll find they don't save as much time as they should.

These days you'll probably opt for an automatic washing machine that fills and empties itself according to a pre-set programme, and so can be left unattended. There is a choice between top loaders and front loaders, although the latter are by far the more common. Obviously top loaders can't fit under a work surface, but drum-type top loaders tend to be narrower and this may suit your particular space requirements.

Dishwashers are almost always automatic, except for some small, cheaper sink-top models. They, too, are available as top or front loaders, though again front loaders are by far the more popular. They are also easier to load and unload, as with top loaders it's easy for crockery and cutlery to slip to the bottom of the machines.

Washing machines have become almost a necessity in busy family homes, especially where there are young children. Dishwashers are far less common, but sales are developing rapidly as more and more people wake up to their advantages. It's a simple matter to stack a dishwasher with dirty crockery direct from the meal table and then turn it on before going to bed at night. Again, for a family the labour saving is considerable.

Some washing machines don't have to be plumbed in. The inlets can be attached to the kitchen taps when the sink isn't being used, and the outlet can be hooked over the edge of the sink. The same goes for dishwashers, which usually require only a cold water feed. But to keep things really neat and tidy as well as more practical, it is best to create permanent connections for both the water supply and the waste outlet. In most kitchens this should be a fairly easy task, provided you have room for the machines in the first place.

As far as the capacities of washing machines and dishwashers go, you don't really have much choice. Washing machines have a capacity of about 4-5kg (9-11lb) and dishwashers will function quite happily provided you stack them up within the obvious tray limitations. It's important to follow the manufacturers' instructions for day-to-day maintenance. Many washing machines need their outlet filter cleaned regularly, as

do dishwashers. They may also need regular doses of salts, not to mention rinse aids.

Water supply

There are a number of ways in which you can arrange the water supply. One of them is sure to suit your plumbing system or the layout of your kitchen or utility room. A washing machine may need a hot and cold supply; dishwashers and some cheaper washing machines need only a cold supply.

Let's first consider the conventional means of plumbing in – the means that a professional plumber would almost certainly adopt if you called him in to do the job for you. It is likely to be most satisfactory where the machine is to be positioned in the immediate vicinity of the kitchen sink and the 15mm (1/2in) hot and cold supply pipes to the sink taps are readily accessible and in close proximity to each other.

The technique is to cut into these two pipes

at a convenient level, after cutting off the water supply and draining the pipes, and to insert into them 15mm compression tees. From the outlets of the tees lengths of 15mm (1/2in) copper tube are run to terminate, against the wall, in a position immediately adjacent to the machine. Onto the ends of these lengths of pipe are fitted purpose-made stop-cocks. These are usually provided with back-plates that can be screwed to the wall after it has been drilled and plugged. The outlets of the stop-cocks are designed for connection to the machine's inlet hose or hoses.

As an alternative, which is best used where the hot and cold water pipes in the kitchen are in close proximity to the position of the machine, you can use a special patent valve. This is a 'tee' with a valve outlet designed for direct connection to the washing machine hose. There are compression joints at each end of the tee and the valve is particularly

PLUMBING IN A WASHING MACHINE

Plumbing in a washing machine shouldn't present too many problems. Normally it's sited next to an existing sink, so you'll know that the water supply pipes and drainage facilities are close at hand.

Most machines are run off separate 15mm (½in) hot and cold supplies (1 & 2) taken from tees (3) inserted in the pipe runs to the sink. You should also insert some form of stop-valve (4) into the pipes so the machine can be isolated for repairs. You'll have to use female/male connections (5) to join the copper pipes to the machine's rubber inlet hoses (6).

When the water has been used, it's fed into a rubber drain hose (7) which should be loosely inserted into the top of the stand-pipe (8). This in turn connects to a 75mm (3in) trap and from here the waste water is taken in 38mm (1½in) pipe to discharge in the gully outside below the grille.

Dealing with single-stack drainage

From the trap at the bottom of the stand-pipe (11) the waste water is conducted to the main drainage stack (12) where the pipe is connected via a fitting known as a strap boss(13).

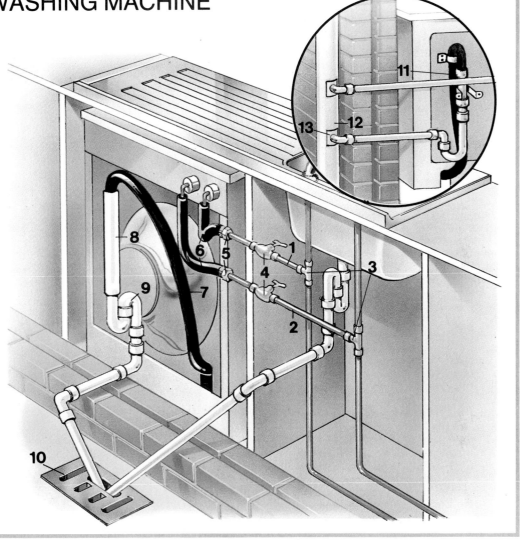

easily fitted because there is no tube-stop in one of these joints. This cuts out the difficult business of 'springing' the cut ends of the pipe into the tee.

Then there are valves which can be connected without cutting a section out of the water supply pipes. With one such valve the pipe is drained and is then drilled with a 8mm (⅝₆in) bit. A back-plate is then fitted to the wall behind it and a front-plate, with a short projecting pipe and a rubber seal that fits into the hole in the pipe, is clamped to it. The washing machine valve then screws into this front-plate.

Yet another valve is self-tapping and screws its own hole in the water pipe. This, so the makers claim, can be done without cutting off the water supply and draining the pipe.

A valve which depends upon drilling the water supply pipe will not permit the same flow of water as one in which the pipe is cut and a tee inserted. It must be said, though,

that this seems to make very little difference in practice, but obviously in the former case the tightening of the connection must be more than sufficient for it to work properly.

Putting in drainage

The simplest method is undoubtedly to hook the machine's outlet hose over the rim of the kitchen or utility room sink when required. However, this method isn't always convenient and is certainly untidy. An alternative is to provide an open-ended stand-pipe fixed to the kitchen wall into which the outlet hose of the machine can be permanently hooked. The open end of the stand-pipe should be at least 600mm (24in) above floor level and should have an internal diameter of at least 35mm (1⅜in). A deep seal (75mm/3in) trap should be provided at its base and a branch waste pipe taken from its outlet to an exterior gully, if on the ground floor, or to the main soil and waste stack of a single stack

system if on an upper floor. As with all connections to a single soil and waste stack this should be done only under the supervision of the district or borough council's Building Control Officer. Manufacturers of plastic drainage systems include suitable drainage stand-pipes and accessories in their range of equipment (the trap and pipe being sold as one unit).

It is sometimes possible to deal with washing machine or dishwasher drainage by taking the waste pipe to connect directly to the trap of the kitchen sink and this course of action may be suggested at DIY centres and by builders' merchants staff. But it must be stressed that this is not recommended by the manufacturers of washing machines, who consider that it involves a considerable risk of back-siphonage. This could lead to waste water from the sink siphoning back into the machine. In the case of a washing machine this could mean considerable problems.

PLUMBING IN A DISHWASHER

1 Start by working out how to run the waste outlet. This will often mean making a hole in the wall using a club hammer and cold chisel.

2 Measure up the run on the inside, then cut a suitable length of 38mm (1¹/₂in) PVC plastic waste pipe and push it through the hole you have made.

3 Make up the outside pipe run dry, to ensure it all fits, then solvent weld it. It's useful to put in an inspection elbow in case of blockages.

6 Carry on assembling the run on the inside using standard waste pipe fittings. Try to keep the run close to the wall for a neat appearance.

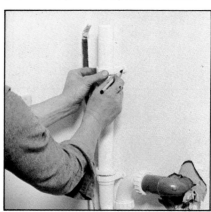

7 Take the trap and stand-pipe, which you can buy as a standard fitting or make up yourself, and mark the bracket positions on the wall.

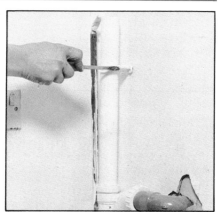

8 Drill and plug the wall, and fix the stand-pipe in position. Make sure that it is fully supported and vertical and the trap is screwed tight.

11 Make good the damage to the wall both on the inside and out; the plastic pipe will be held firmly in place by the mortar and plaster.

12 You can now move the machine into position and connect it up. The inlet hose has a female screwed connector, which must have a washer in it.

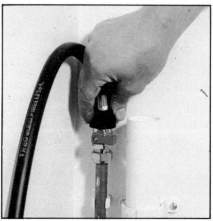

13 With the washer in place, screw up the connector to the tap on the inlet pipe; it's enough to hand-tighten this connection.

4 If the run terminates in a gully drain, then make sure that you fit the pipe so that the end is situated below the level of the water.

5 When you have completed the outside waste run, replace the grid. Cut away as much of it as necessary to fit round the pipe, using a hacksaw.

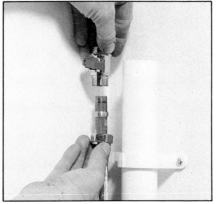

9 Run the cold water supply using 15mm (½in) pipe via a tee cut into tne domestic cold supply, and attach a running tap to the end.

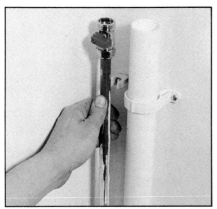

10 Secure the supply pipe to the wall using pipe brackets, then go back and make sure that all your connections are sound.

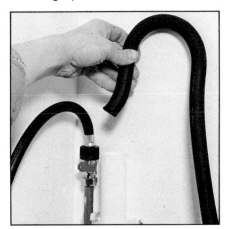

14 Take the outlet hose from the machine and place it in the top of the stand-pipe.You should not attempt to make the connection airtight.

15 Move the machine exactly into position and check that it is level; if not, adjust the feet. Then turn on the water and test the machine.

Ready Reference

INSTALLATION CHECKLIST

When installing a washing machine or dishwasher, remember that:
- it's usual to take the water supply from the domestic cold water system; if you want to use the mains you may need a pressure reducer, so check with the manufacturer's literature
- if the machine takes a hot and cold supply you will have to ensure that there is sufficient pressure in the hot supply and that this is the same as that from the cold
- to operate at maximum efficiency, the machine should stand on a level surface and this should be firm; washing machines in particular are extremely heavy when full of water.

BATHROOM REGULATIONS

If you want to put your washing machine in the bathroom then there are electrical rules that must be obeyed:
- it must be permanently wired in
- you must not be able to touch the controls when you're in the bath or shower.

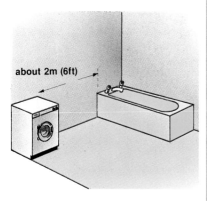

TIP: CHECK DIMENSIONS

If the machine is going to be put between existing units or under a work surface you'll have to measure up carefully before you buy. Make sure there is enough space behind for the plumbing work.

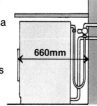

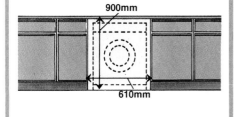

PLUMBING IN A BATH

**Replacing a bath may seem to be an ambitious do-it-yourself project but it is well within the capabilities of the determined home handyman prepared to tackle the job carefully and logically.
Here is what is involved.**

As with many other plumbing projects the most difficult part is likely to be the removal of the old fitting rather than the installation of the new one.

The old bath will almost certainly be made of enamelled cast iron. The once-white enamel may be discoloured and wearing away, and may even reveal rusting bare metal underneath. Green or brown coloured stains beneath the taps indicate a long-neglected need for rewashering. The taps may look out of date and have worn chromium plating. The finish of the bath may be old and unattractive and the bath itself not panelled in.

Checking it out

First have a look at the existing bath. If there are side or end panels, strip them off and examine, with the aid of an electric torch, the water supply pipes and the waste and the overflow arrangements in the cramped and badly lit space between the foot of the bath and the wall. You will see that the water supply pipes connect the threaded tails of the taps by means of brass 'swivel tap connectors' or 'cap and lining joints'.

Check whether the water supply pipes are made of copper or lead by scraping their surface with the blade of a pocket knife. If this reveals the characteristic grey sheen of lead you should think of replacing the piping. If you *do* want to retain the lead piping you will have to call in a qualified plumber – it's not an easy task. If the pipes are of copper you should be able to tackle the entire project without professional aid.

The overflow from a modern bath is taken, by means of a flexible pipe, to the waste trap. In the past, the overflow pipe often simply led through the external wall, and was the source of incurable bathroom draughts. If your bath's overflow is like this, you'll have to cut it off flush with the wall.

If the bath has adjustable feet, apply some penetrating oil to the screws. Once they begin to move, lowering the level of the bath before you attempt to remove it can help to prevent damage to the wall tiling.

The alternatives

It is possible to replace your cast iron bath with a new one made of the same material, but more modern in styling. However, these baths are expensive and very heavy indeed. Carrying one into the bathroom and fitting it requires considerable strength (you'd need at least one strong helper) as well as care. There are other snags about enamelled cast iron baths. They normally have a slippery base that can make them dangerous to use – particularly by the very young and the elderly, though some are available with a non-slip surface. Furthermore, the material of which they are made rapidly conducts the heat away from the water and while this didn't matter too much in the days when energy was plentiful and cheap, large amounts of hot water cost rather more today.

One economical alternative is an enamelled pressed steel bath. This is lighter and cheaper than enamelled cast iron but can be more easily damaged in storage or installation.

For do-it-yourself installation a plastic bath is the obvious choice. These are made of acrylic plastic sheet, sometimes reinforced with glass fibre. They are available in a number of attractive colours and, as the colour extends right through the material of which they are made, any surface scratches can be easily polished out. They are light in weight and one

man can quite easily carry one upstairs for installation. The plastic of which they are made is a poor conductor of heat which means that they are both comfortable and economical to use. Many of them have a non-slip base to make them safe.

But plastic baths do have their snags. They are easily damaged by extreme heat. You should be beware of using a blow torch in proximity to one and a lighted cigarette should never be rested, even momentarily, on the rim. A fault of early plastic baths was their tendency to creak and sag when filled with hot water and, sometimes, when you got into them. This has now been overcome by the manufacturers who provide substantial frames or cradles for support; but these frames must be assembled and fixed exactly as recommended. Some come already attached to the bath.

A combined plastic waste and overflow assembly is likely to be the choice nowadays for any bath, and is obligatory with a plastic bath. If a rigid metal trap is used with a plastic bath, the material of the bath could be damaged as hot water causes unequal expansion.

You obviously won't want to re-use the old bath taps and will probably opt for either individual modern ¾in bath pillar taps or a bath mixer. A mixer should be chosen only if the cold water supply is taken from the same cold

REPOSITIONING A BATH

In many bathrooms, a new bath simply takes the place of an existing one; there's no room for manoeuvre. But in some cases moving the bath to another position in the room can lead to a more practical arrangement and better use of the available space. In this bathroom the new bath was installed at the other side of the

room, so that the space it had formerly occupied could house a shower cubicle and a WC. Moving the bath to this position involved extending the existing hot and cold water supply pipes, but brought it nearer the soil stack on the outside wall and meant that the waste pipe was short and simple to connect up outside.

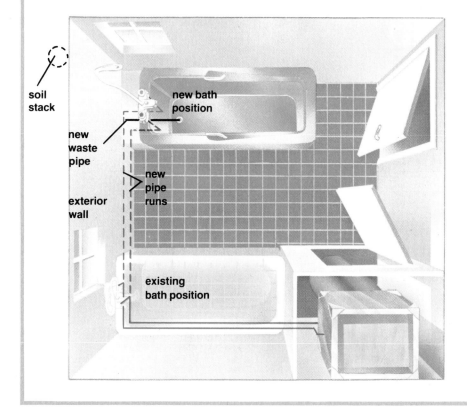

Ready Reference

EQUIPMENT ROUND-UP

To replace a bath, you're likely to need the following tools:
- crowsfoot wrench
- adjustable spanner
- adjustable wrench
- hacksaw (possibly)
- spirit level

You'll also need:
- new bath — measure up carefully before you buy it to make sure it fits. It should come complete with supports, carcase and side panels, otherwise you'll need these as well
- new overflow connection, waste outlet and PVC trap
- taps/mixer and new inlet pipe if you are replacing them
- plumber's putty

KNOW YOUR BATH

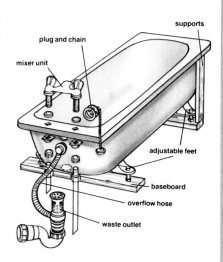

THE SPACE YOU NEED

You need a minimum amount of space around a bath (below) and also a minimum ceiling height above it (right).

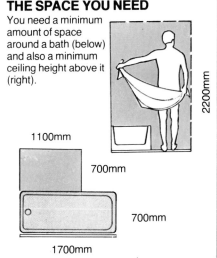

water storage cistern that supplies the hot water system. It should not be used where the cold water supply to the bathroom comes directly from the mains supply.

How to proceed

To avoid too long a disruption of the domestic hot and cold water supplies you can fit the taps, waste and trap into the new bath before removing the old one.

Slip a flat plastic washer over the tail of each tap and insert the tails through the holes provided for them. A mixer usually has one large flat washer or gasket with two holes — one for each tap tail. Beneath the rim of the bath, slip 'top hat' or 'spacer' washers over the tails to accommodate the protruding shanks of the taps. Screw on the back-nuts and tighten them. For details, see pages 57 to 59.

Bed the waste flange onto plumber's putty or non-setting mastic, secure the back-nut

and connect up the trap. Then connect up the overflow pipe.

Removing the old bath may well be the most difficult part of the procedure. Turn off the hot and cold water supplies and drain the distribution pipes from the bath taps. If you haven't done so already, remove the bath panel to give access to the plumbing at the foot of the bath. You can try to unscrew the back-nuts holding the taps in position, but it's generally easier to undo the nuts that connect the distribution pipes to the tails of the taps. In order to reach the one nearest the wall you may have to dismantle the overflow, either by unscrewing it or, if it is taken through the wall, by cutting it off flush with the wall. Then undo the waste connection.

The bath is now disconnected from the water supply pipes and from the branch waste pipe and can be pulled away from the wall. Unless you particularly want to save the old bath and have some strong helpers, do not attempt to remove it from the room or the house in one piece. It is very heavy. The best course of action is to break it into manageable pieces. Drape an old blanket over it to prevent flying chips of enamel and wear goggles to protect the eyes. Then, with a club hammer, break the bath up into pieces that you can easily carry away.

Place the new plastic bath in position and assemble the cradle or other support exactly as recommended by the manufacturer. It is most unlikely that the tails of the new taps will coincide with the position of the tap connectors of the old distribution pipes. If they don't, the easiest way of making the connections is by means of bendable copper pipe. This is corrugated copper tubing – easily bent by hand. It is obtainable in 15mm and 22mm sizes and either with two plain ends for connection to soldered capillary or compression joints, or with one plain end and a swivel tap connector at the other. For this particular job two lengths of 22mm corrugated copper pipe will be required, each with one end plain and one end fitted with a swivel tap connector.

Offer the corrugated pipe lengths up to the tap tails and cut back the distribution pipes to the length required for connection to the plain ends. Leave these pipes slightly too long rather than too short. The corrugated pipe can be bent to accommodate a little extra length. Now connect the plain ends to the cut distribution pipes using either soldered capillary or Type 'A' compression couplings.

The chances are that the distribution pipes will be ¾in imperial size. If you use compression fittings an adaptor — probably simply a larger olive — will be needed for connection to a 22mm coupling. If you use soldered capillary fittings, special ¾in to 22mm couplings must be used. Remember to keep the blowtorch flame well away from the plastic of the bath. Connect up the swivel tap connectors of the corrugated pipe and the overflow of the bath. Do this in a logical order. First connect the tap connector to the further tap. A fibre washer inside the nut of the tap connector will ensure a watertight joint. Then connect up the flexible overflow pipe of the combined waste-and-overflow fitting to the bath's overflow outlet. Finally connect the nearer tap to the nearer tap connector.

If you have installed new pipework then you can install the entire trap, waste and water supply pipe spurs before moving the bath into position. Whatever you have decided upon, finish making all the connections, then reinstate the water supply and check for leaks.

The level of the positioned bath should now be checked using a spirit level, and adjustments made (you'll need a spanner to set the adjustable feet). When all is level, fit the side and end panels in position and the job is finished.

TAKING OUT THE OLD BATH

1 Think about how you're going to get the old bath out before you begin. The connections are likely to be inaccessible, old and corroded.

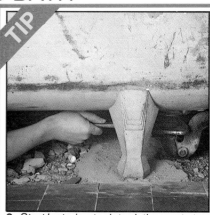

2 Start by trying to detach the waste trap using an adjustable wrench and, if necessary, penetrating oil.

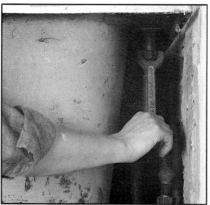

3 Undo the back-nuts underneath the taps or mixer. These are likely to be more difficult to undo than the trap; use a crowsfoot wrench.

4 If the back-nuts won't undo you may have to detach the supply pipes at another joint. Use an adjustable spanner to undo the nut.

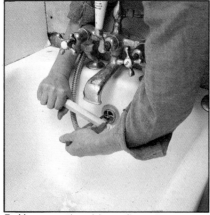

5 Unscrew the old overflow pipe. Alternatively you can simply saw off both supply and overflow pipes — but you'll need to install new ones.

6 When the bath is free, drag it out of position. You'll need at least one other person to help you get a cast iron bath out unless you break it up first.

ATTACHING THE NEW FITTINGS

1 Start to assemble the new plumbing. Wind PTFE tape around the screw thread of the waste outlet and spread some plumber's putty underneath the rim.

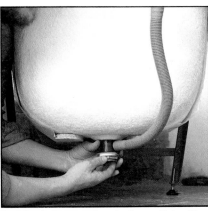

3 Attach the overflow to the outlet with a locking nut and a plastic O ring, which is inserted between them. Screw up the nut and tighten gently.

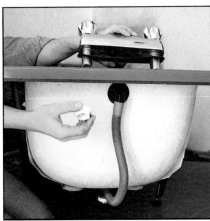

5 Take the mixer and check that the rubber gasket is in position between the unit and the bath, and also that it is clean and free from bits of grit.

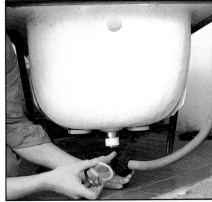

2 Put the waste outlet in position and make sure that it is firmly seated. These days the overflow will be made of plastic and connects to the waste outlet.

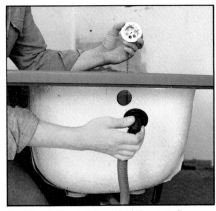

4 Attach the inlet end of the overflow which will have the plug and chain attached to it. Screw it into the pipe connector and tighten it up.

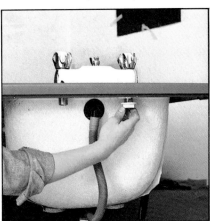

6 Screw the back-nuts up onto the trap and tighten them. Insert a flat plastic washer or top hat washer between the nut and the bath.

Ready Reference

BATH TYPES
Most baths sold today have outside dimensions of about 1675mm (66in) long, 750mm (30in) wide, and 550mm (21in) high. Shorter baths are available for particularly small bathrooms and these are roughly 1525mm (60in) and 1375mm (54in) long. Other baths may be up to 1825mm (72in) long and 1100mm (43in) wide. They also come in different bottom mouldings to make them safe and often have handles to help the less active get in and out. Although most are basically rectangular inside and out some are oval-shaped and designed to fit into corners. There are also special baths for the disabled which are much shorter and formed in the shape of a seat.

Plain traditional rectangular

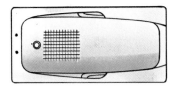

Off-rectangular with handles

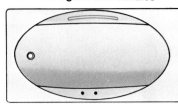

Large oval with side plumbing

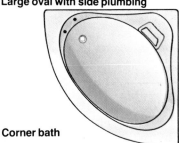

Corner bath

Disabled bath

INSTALLING THE NEW BATH

1 If you have installed new pipework, you should attach inlet spurs to the taps before you have to install the bath in its final position.

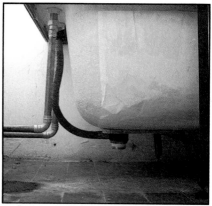

2 Put the bath into position. You may want to stand it away from the wall at the front end so that you can build in a shelf. Connect the inlet pipes.

3 Fit the waste trap and attach it to the waste pipe. When all the pipework is connected up, turn on the water and check for leaks.

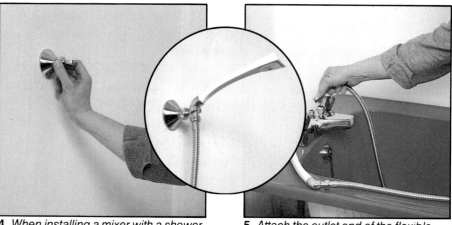

4 When installing a mixer with a shower attachment, fix the shower head bracket to the wall and fit the shower head into the bracket (inset).

5 Attach the outlet end of the flexible shower hose to central outlet on the mixer unit. It should plug in and click into position with a slight turn.

6 Check that the bath is level both lengthways and widthways with a spirit level. Adjust the screwed-on feet to get the level right.

7 Fix the bath panels in position by screwing them to the wooden carcase which surrounds the bath and is supplied by the manufacturer.

8 Screw the panels on carefully. They will usually be made of moulded high impact polystyrene which is easily chipped around the screw holes.

9 When all the bath work is complete you will have to make good the décor. If possible tile around the bath and box in the pipework.

REPLACING A WASHBASIN

Replacing a washbasin is fairly straightforward. It's a job you'll have to undertake if the basin is cracked – but you may also want to change the basin if you're redesigning your bathroom and adding some up-to-date fittings.

A part from replacing a cracked basin, which you should do immediately, the most common time to install a new basin is when you're improving a bathroom or decorating a separate WC. The chances are that the basin you'll be removing will be one of the older ceramic types, wall-hung, a pedestal model or built into a vanity unit.

The main advantage of a wall-hung basin is that it doesn't take up any floor space and because of this it is very useful in a small bathroom, WC or cloakroom. You can also set the basin at a comfortable height, unlike a pedestal basin the height of which is fixed by the height of the pedestal. However, it's usual to fit a wall-hung basin with the rim 800mm (32in) above the floor.

Vanity units are now increasing in popularity. In fact they're the descendents of the Edwardian wash-stand, with its marble top, bowl and large water jug. The unit is simply a storage cupboard with a ceramic, enamelled pressed steel or plastic basin set flush in the top. The advantage of vanity units is that you have a counter surface round the basin on which to stand toiletries. There is rarely, if ever, sufficient room for these items behind or above conventional wall-hung or pedestal basins. Usually the top has some form of plastic covering or can be tiled for easy cleaning.

Fittings for basins

It's a good idea to choose the taps and waste fittings at the same time you select the basin, so everything matches. You could perhaps re-use the taps from the old basin, but it's doubtful if these will be in keeping with the design of the new appliance. As an alternative to shrouded head or pillar taps, you could fit a mixer, provided the holes at the back of the basin are suitably spaced to take the tap tails. But remember that because of the design of most basin mixers, you shouldn't use them if the cold water supply is directly from the mains.

Ceramic basins normally have a built-in overflow channel which in most appliances connects into the main outlet above the trap. So if you accidentally let the basin overfill you reduce the risk of water spillage.

PUTTING IN A NEW BASIN

You should have little trouble installing a new washbasin in the same place as the old one. It's also a good opportunity to check the pipe runs. If they're made of lead it's a good idea to replace them.

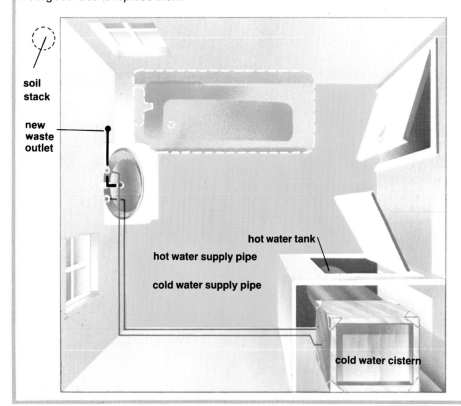

soil stack

new waste outlet

hot water tank

hot water supply pipe

cold water supply pipe

cold water cistern

Vanity unit basins are usually sold complete with a waste and overflow unit which resembles that of a modern stainless steel sink. A flexible tube connects the overflow outlet of the basin with a sleeve or 'banjo' unit which fits tightly round a slotted waste fitting.

With both types of basin the flange of the waste outlet has to be bedded into the hole provided for it in the basin on a layer of plumber's putty. The thread of the screwed waste must also be smeared with jointing compound to ensure a watertight seal where the 'banjo' connects to it.

Traps

The outlet of the waste must, of course, connect to a trap and branch waste pipe. At one time it was the practice to use 'shallow seal' traps with a 50mm (2in) depth of seal for two-pipe drainage systems, and 'deep seal' traps with a 75mm (3in) depth of seal for single stack systems. Today, however, deep seal traps are always fitted.

Of course, the modern bottle trap is one of the most common types used. It's neater looking and requires less space than a traditional U-trap. Where it's concealed behind a pedestal or in a vanity unit you can use one made of plastic, but there are chromium-plated and brass types if you have a wall-hung basin where trap and waste will be clearly visible. The one drawback with bottle traps is that they discharge water more slowly than a U-trap. You can now also buy traps with telescopic inlets that make it easy to provide a push-fit connection to an existing copper or plastic branch waste pipe (see page 18).

Connecting up the water supply

It's unlikely that you'll be able to take out the old basin and install a new one without making some modification to the pipework. It's almost certain that the tap holes will be in a different position. To complicate matters further, taps are now made with shorter tails so you'll probably have to extend the supply pipes by a short length.

If you're installing new supply pipes, how you run them will depend on the type of basin you're putting in. With a wall-hung basin or the pedestal type, the hot and cold pipes are usually run neatly together up the back wall and then bent round to the tap tails. But as a vanity unit will conceal the plumbing there's no need to run the pipes together.

You might find it difficult to bend the required angles, so an easy way round the problem is to use flexible corrugated copper pipe which you can bend by hand to the shape you need. You can buy the pipe with a swivel tap connector at one end and a plain connector, on which you can use capillary or

FITTING A VANITY UNIT

1 Cut a hole in the vanity unit with the help of the template provided or, if the hole is precut, check the measurement against that of the sink.

2 Prop the basin up while you install the mixer unit. Start with the outlet spout which is fixed with a brass nut and packing washers.

5 Now complete the tap heads by first sliding on the flange which covers up the securing nut; next put on the headwork and tighten the retaining nut.

6 Finish off the tap assembly by fitting the coloured markers into place (red for hot is usually on the left), and gently pressing home the chrome cap.

9 Before you put the basin into its final position put a strip of mastic around the opening in the vanity unit to ensure a watertight seal.

10 Press the basin gently into position and fix it to the underside of the top of the vanity unit. Attach the waste plug to its keeper.

3 Now take the water inlet assembly and check that the hot and cold spur pipes are the right length so that the tap sub-assemblies are correctly positioned.

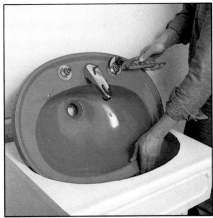

4 Fix the assembly in position with the brass nuts supplied by the manufacturer. Make sure that all the washers are included otherwise the fitting won't be secure.

7 Now insert the waste outlet. Make sure the rubber flange is fitted properly and seats comfortably into the basin surround.

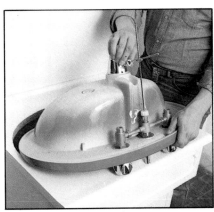

8 Turn the basin over; secure the outlet and the pop-up waste control rods. These may need shortening depending on clearance inside the vanity unit.

11 Now fix the inlet pipes to the two mixer connections and screw on the waste trap. Take the doors off the vanity unit to make access easier.

12 Turn the water back on and check for leaks. Check the pop-up waste system works, then put the doors of the vanity unit back on.

Ready Reference

BASIN SIZES

On basins, the dimension from side to side is specified as the length, and that from back to front as the width.

Most standard sized basins are between 550 and 700mm (22 and 28in) long, and 450 to 500mm (18 to 20in) wide.

BASIN COMPONENTS

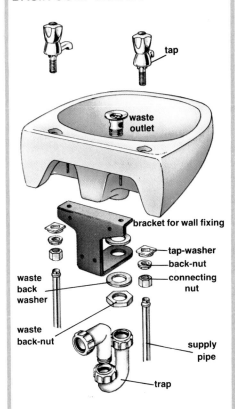

THE SPACE YOU'LL NEED

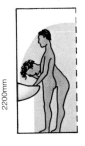

Think about the space around your basin particularly if you are installing a new one. You not only need elbow room when you are bending over it, such as when you are washing your hair, but also room in front to stand back – especially if you put a mirror above it. Here are the recommended dimensions for the area around your basin.

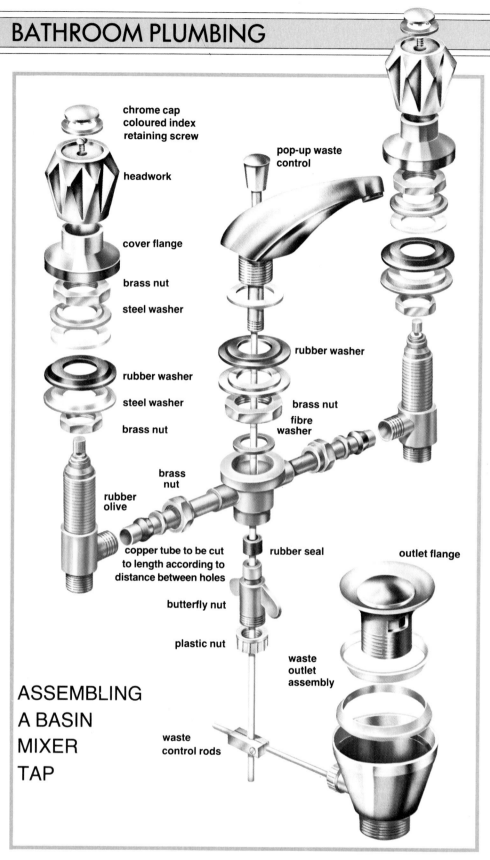

chrome cap
coloured index
retaining screw

headwork

cover flange

brass nut

steel washer

rubber washer

steel washer

brass nut

rubber olive

brass nut

copper tube to be cut to length according to distance between holes

pop-up waste control

rubber washer

brass nut
fibre washer

rubber seal

outlet flange

butterfly nut

plastic nut

waste outlet assembly

waste control rods

ASSEMBLING A BASIN MIXER TAP

When fitting the taps all you have to do is to remove the back-nuts and slip flat plastic washers over the tails (if they aren't there already). The taps can then be positioned in the holes in the basin. When this has been done more plastic washers (or top hat washers) have to be slipped over the tails before the back-nuts are replaced. It's important not to overtighten these as it's quite easy to damage a ceramic basin.

Because some vanity unit basins are made of a thinner material, you may find that the shanks of the taps fitted into them will protrude below the under-surface of the basin. The result is that when the back-nut is fully tightened, it still isn't tight against the underside of the basin. To get round the problem you have to fit a top hat washer over the shank so the back-nut can be screwed up against it.

Mixers usually have one large washer or gasket between the base of the mixer and the top of the basin and you fix them in exactly the same way.

When you've fitted the taps you can then fit the waste. With a ceramic basin you'll have to use a slotted waste to enable water from the overlfow to escape into the drainage pipe. Getting this in place means first removing the back-nut so you can slip it through the outlet hole in the basin – which itself should be coated with a generous layer of plumber's putty. It's essential to make sure that the slot in the waste fitting coincides with the outlet of the basin's built-in overflow. You'll then have to smear jointing compound on the protruding screw thread of the tail, slip on a plastic washer and replace and tighten the back-nut. As you do this the waste flange will probably try to turn on its seating, but you can prevent this by holding the grid with pliers as you tighten the back-nut.

Finally, any excess putty that is squeezed out as the flange is tightened against the basin should be wiped away.

A vanity unit will probably be supplied with a combined waste and overflow unit. This is a flexible hose that has to be fitted (unlike a ceramic basin, where it's an integral part of the appliance). The slotted waste is bedded in exactly the same way as a waste on a ceramic basin. You then have to fit one end of the overflow to the basin outlet and slip the 'banjo' outlet on the other end over the tail of the waste to cover the slot. It's held in position by a washer and back-nut.

Fitting the basin
Once the taps and waste have been fixed in position on the new basin, you should be ready to remove the old basin and fit the new one in its place. First you need to cut off the water supply to the basin, either by turning off the main stop-valve (or any gate valve on

compression fittings at the other. If you're using ordinary copper pipe, the easiest way to start is by bending the pipe to the correct angle first, and then cutting the pipe to the right length at each end afterwards. See pages 25 to 27.

Preparing the basin
Before you fix the basin in position, you'll need to fit the taps (or mixer) and the waste. It's much easier to do this at this stage than later when the basin is against the wall because you will have more room to manoeuvre in.

the distribution pipes) or by tying up the ball-valve supplying the main cold water storage cistern. Then open the taps and leave them until the water ceases to flow. If the existing basin is a pedestal model you'll have to remove the pedestal which may be screwed to the floor. Take off the nut that connects the basin trap to the threaded waste outlet and unscrew the nuts that connect the water supply pipes to the tails of the taps. These will either be swivel tap connectors or cap and lining joints. You'll need to be able to lift the basin clear and then remove the brackets or hangers on which it rests.

You'll probably need some help when installing the new basin as it's much easier to mark the fixing holes if someone else is holding the basin against the wall. With a pedestal basin, the pedestal will determine the level of the basin. The same applies with a vanity unit. But if the basin is set on hangers or brackets, you can adjust the height for convenience.

Once the fixing holes have been drilled and plugged, the basin can be screwed into position and you can deal with the plumbing. Before you make the connections to the water supply pipes you may have to cut or lengthen them to meet the tap tails. If you need to lengthen them you'll find it easier to use corrugated copper pipe. The actual connection between pipe and tail is made with a swivel tap connector – a form of compression fitting.

Finally you have to connect the trap. You may be able to re-use the old one, but it's more likely you'll want to fit a new one. And if its position doesn't coincide with the old one, you can use a bottle trap with an adjustable telescopic inlet.

FITTING A PEDESTAL BASIN

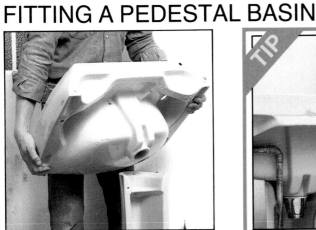

1 Stand the basin on the pedestal to check the height of the water supply pipe runs and the outlet. Measure the height of the wall fixing points.

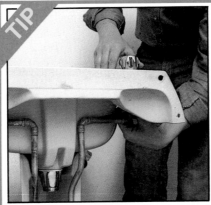

2 When you're making up the pipe run to connect to the tap tails, plan it so the pipes are neatly concealed within the body of the pedestal.

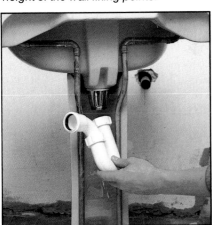

3 Line up the piped waste outlet and fix the trap to the basin outlet. A telescopic trap may be useful here to adjust for a varying level.

4 Move the whole unit into its final position, screw the basin to the wall, connect the waste trap to the outlet, and connect up the supply pipes.

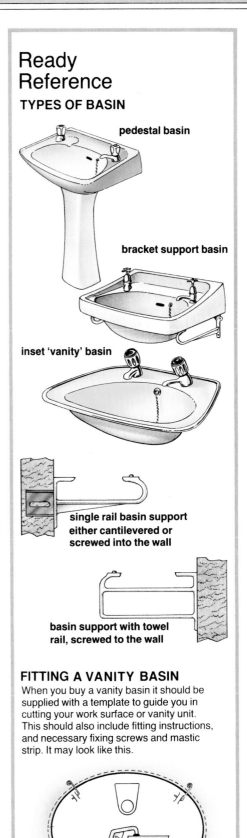

Ready Reference

TYPES OF BASIN

pedestal basin

bracket support basin

inset 'vanity' basin

single rail basin support either cantilevered or screwed into the wall

basin support with towel rail, screwed to the wall

FITTING A VANITY BASIN

When you buy a vanity basin it should be supplied with a template to guide you in cutting your work surface or vanity unit. This should also include fitting instructions, and necessary fixing screws and mastic strip. It may look like this.

REPLACING YOUR WC

Replacing your WC need not be a frightening prospect provided you follow a few basic rules. It also gives you the opportunity to install a quieter and more efficient piece of equipment.

There are several reasons why you may wish to remove and replace your WC suite. The existing pan may be cracked, in which case replacement must not be delayed, and no attempt should be made to repair it. Or the porcelain may be crazed making it unsightly, and difficult to keep clean. Most likely, however, the reason will be that your existing WC is simply old fashioned and due for replacement as part of an overall improvement plan.

Pan or cistern?
If it's just the pan you find fault with then that's all you need to replace. Colours for sanitary-ware, as WCs are usually called by the manufacturers, are fairly standardised, and you should have no difficulty in obtaining a pan to match the existing cistern.

If, on the other hand, you want to convert an old-fashioned lavatory suite with a high-level cistern, it may be possible to replace only the flushing cistern and flush pipe (or 'flush bend' as it is often called) with a low level one, while keeping the existing pan.

However, in order to accommodate the flushing cistern, the pans of low level suites are usually positioned 25 to 50mm (1 to 2in) further from the wall behind the suite than are those of high level ones. If you overlook this point you are likely to find that the seat and cover of the pan cannot be raised properly when the new cistern is fitted.

Slim-line cisterns
In recent years manufacturers have developed slim-line flushing cisterns or 'flush panels' only about 115mm (4¼in) deep. These can, in most cases, be used to convert a WC from high level to low level operation without moving the pan. With such a cistern the flushing inlet to the pan can be as little as 130mm (5¼in) from the wall behind, instead of the 200 to 230 (8 to 9in) required by an ordinary low level cistern. To make room for the full 9 litres (2 gal) of water needed for an adequate flush, these slimline cisterns are rather wider from side to side than conventional ones. So make sure that there is sufficient unobstructed width of wall behind the suite to accommodate it.

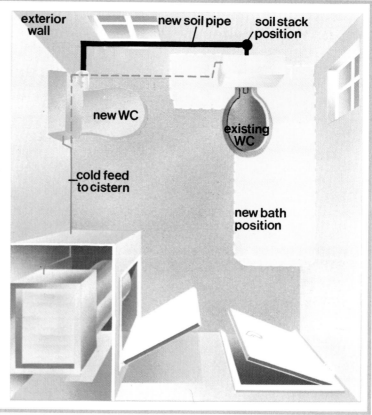

PLANNING THE MOVE

The biggest problem concerns the position of the soil stack. In this bathroom the old soil pipe was disconnected, and a new soil pipe run was installed on the outside of the bathroom wall to link the new WC to the existing soil stack. This was much neater than running the new pipe inside the bathroom, where it would have had to be boxed in.

The other alteration to existing pipework involved cutting the cold feed to the cistern part-way along its run, and re-connecting it to the new cistern.

exterior wall — new soil pipe — soil stack position — new WC — existing WC — cold feed to cistern — new bath position

Siphonic suites

Close-coupled lavatory suites, in which the pan and cistern form one unit without even the short flush bend of a low level cistern, are neater in appearance than the other kinds. They are particularly silent and effective where they are flushed and cleansed by siphonic action, as distinct from the 'wash down' action in which flushing simply releases the full contents of the cistern into the pan, and the weight of water carries away its contents. They also provide a larger water surface area than older pans, an important factor in maintaining the cleanliness of the pan.

There are two kinds of siphonic suite, single-trap and double-trap. The single-trap pattern is the simpler and cheaper. The outlet is first constricted and then widened to connect to the branch drain or soil pipe. When the suite is flushed, water completely fills the restricted section of the outlet and passes on, taking air with it, to create a partial vacuum. Atmospheric pressure then pushes the contents of the pan into the drain. The siphonic action is broken, often with a gurgle, as air passes under the bend of the trap.

With a double-trap siphonic suite a specially designed air pipe or 'pressure reducer' connects the air space between the two traps to the channel through which the flushing water passes. As this water flows past the pressure reducer it sucks up air from the space between the two traps, in the same way that the wind passing over the top of a chimney sucks up air from a room below. It's this that creates the partial vacuum on which siphonic action depends. Where a double-trap siphonic suite is working properly, you'll see the water level in the pan fall before the 'flush' water flows in. Although more expensive than other kinds, these suites are valuable where, as in an entrance lobby cloakroom for instance, silent operation is a prime consideration.

Just as low level WC suites normally project further from the wall behind them than high level ones, close-coupled suites project further than either. Don't forget this when considering the provision of such a suite in a small bathroom or cloakroom. You may have to change the position of the washbasin and this, in turn, could obstruct the door.

Pan fixings

Moving an existing WC pan isn't always easy. It's likely to depend largely upon whether it is installed upstairs or on the ground floor. Upstairs WCs usually have a P-trap outlet, which is almost horizontal and is connected to a branch soil pipe by means of a putty or mortar joint. This can easily be broken with a club hammer and cold chisel once you have disconnected the pan from the floor.

Downstairs WCs usually have their bases firmly cemented to a solid floor and usually have an S-trap outlet which is vertical. This connects via a cement joint to an earthenware drain socket protruding above floor level. To remove such a pan it's necessary to break the outlet. Use a cold chisel to detach the front part of the pan from the floor, then use a cold chisel and hammer again to clear the pan outlet and the joining material from the drain socket.

Nowadays it is usual to connect both ground floor and upstairs WCs to the soil pipe using a flexible joint, usually a patent plastic push-fit joint with a spigot that is inserted into the drain and a 'finned' socket that fits over the WC pan outlet.

Such patent joins are nowadays manufactured in a range that covers virtually any WC installation. Not only are they easy to use but they help reduce the noise of a flushing lavatory. It's not considered to be good practice today to cement the base of a WC to a solid floor, as the setting of the cement can create stresses resulting in a cracked pan. It is best to remove every trace of cement from the floor and, having achieved a dead-level base, to secure the WC pan with screws driven into plugs pushed into holes drilled in the floor.

How to start

After you have turned off the water supply and flushed the cistern to empty it, the next step is to disconnect the cistern's water supply, overflow and outlet pipes. So begin by unscrewing the cap-nut connecting the water-supply pipe to the cistern's ball-valve inlet. Then undo the back-nut retaining the cistern's overflow or warning pipe. Finally undo the large nut which secures the threaded outlet of the cistern to the flush pipe. It should now be possible to lift the old cistern off its supporting bracket or brackets.

If the WC suite is a very old one and screwed to a timber floor, unscrew and remove the pan's fixing screws. Then, taking the pan in both hands, pull it from side to side and away from the wall. If the connection to the soil pipe is made with a mastic or putty joint, the pan outlet should come easily out of its socket (which will have to be cleaned of all jointing material before the new unit is fitted). If a rigid cement joint has been used then there's usually no alternative but to use a bit of force. This means deliberately breaking the pan outlet, just behind the trap and above the pipe socket, with a club hammer. You can then prise the front part of the pan away from the floor using a cold chisel and hammer. This will separate the pan outlet from the pipe. At this point it's a

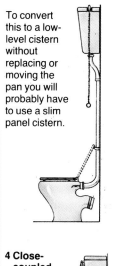
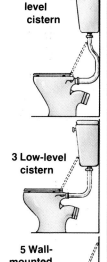

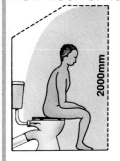

REMOVING THE OLD PAN

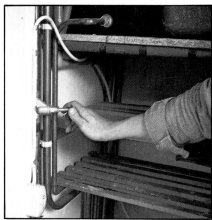

1 Locate the water pipe which supplies the WC cistern and completely shut off the stop valve which controls it. If no valve exists, block the cistern outlet.

2 Lift the top off the cistern and then press the flush handle to empty it. No more fresh water should flow in as the ball float falls.

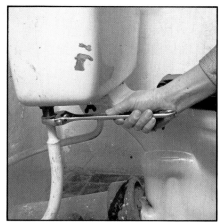

3 Disconnect the overflow pipe. If it is made of lead you should replace it with a PVC pipe run. Saw it off if you are repositioning the WC elsewhere.

4 Disconnect the supply pipe in the same way as the overflow. If you are replacing the piping altogether, you can cut through it with a hacksaw.

5 Disconnect the cistern from the pan. A close-coupled one is lifted off; with other suites you may have to disconnect the flush pipe between cistern and pan.

6 Unscrew the pan from the floor, and then use a hammer and cold chisel to break the joint between the pan and the outlet, tapping gently but firmly.

7 When you have fractured the joint, ease the pan away from the pipe. Even if it is bedded on mortar it should come away easily. Chip away the old mortar.

8 Dispose of the pan and extract any loose bits of debris from the socket. Stuff newspaper into the opening to stop bits falling into the soil pipe.

9 If you are going to use the pipe again clean it out carefully, ready to be connected up to the new WC pan with a proprietary connector.

INSTALLING THE NEW PAN

1 Offer up the pan to the outlet (note that here a new PVC soil pipe has been installed). When it fits snugly, mark down the positions for the fixing screws.

2 Drill the holes and reposition the pan and cistern. Fit the pan outlet into the white push-fit adaptor so that it is firmly in position.

3 Secure the cistern to the wall with screws and plugs. Then attach the new overflow pipe, finally tightening up the lock-nut with an adjustable spanner.

4 Assemble the internal flushing mechanism, see Ready Reference. Attach the water supply pipe and the flushing handle.

5 Fit the seat assembly, making sure that the gaskets are correctly in place between the seat and the pan; screw up the nuts tightly.

6 Restore the water supply. Check that the cistern fills to the correct level and adjust the ball-valve if it does not. Finally flush to fill the pan trap.

Ready Reference

CISTERN MECHANISMS

There are two sorts of flushing mechanism the bell type in well-bottom cisterns and the piston type found otherwise. The latter is by far the more popular today.

well-bottom cistern for replacement of high-level arrangements

lever flush cistern for low-level suite

slim-line flush panel where depth is restricted – usually when a high-level arrangement is converted to a low-level one

THE FLUSH MECHANISM

You'll find you have to assemble the mechanism which is bagged up inside the new cistern. Lay out the components (A) and check them against the enclosed instruction leaflet before assembling them correctly (B).

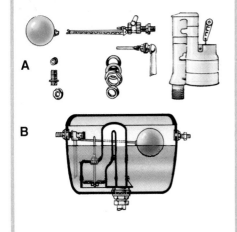

A

B

For more information on WCs see the following section.

THREE TYPES OF WC

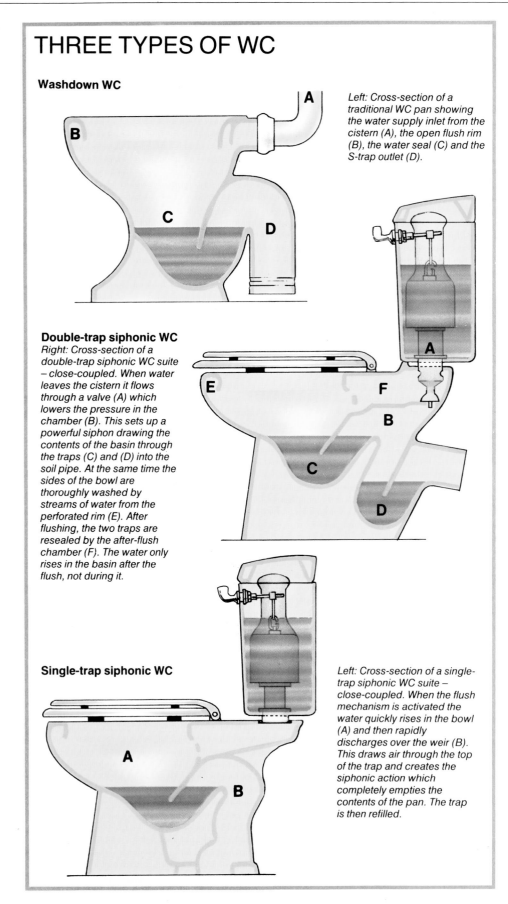

Washdown WC

Left: Cross-section of a traditional WC pan showing the water supply inlet from the cistern (A), the open flush rim (B), the water seal (C) and the S-trap outlet (D).

Double-trap siphonic WC
Right: Cross-section of a double-trap siphonic WC suite – close-coupled. When water leaves the cistern it flows through a valve (A) which lowers the pressure in the chamber (B). This sets up a powerful siphon drawing the contents of the basin through the traps (C) and (D) into the soil pipe. At the same time the sides of the bowl are thoroughly washed by streams of water from the perforated rim (E). After flushing, the two traps are resealed by the after-flush chamber (F). The water only rises in the basin after the flush, not during it.

Single-trap siphonic WC

Left: Cross-section of a single-trap siphonic WC suite – close-coupled. When the flush mechanism is activated the water quickly rises in the bowl (A) and then rapidly discharges over the weir (B). This draws air through the top of the trap and creates the siphonic action which completely empties the contents of the pan. The trap is then refilled.

good idea to stuff a bundle of rags or screwed-up newspaper into the drain socket to prevent any debris getting into the soil pipe. Next attack the socket to remove the remains of the pan's outlet. For this, use a small cold chisel and hammer but do it carefully to avoid damaging the drain socket itself – this will be used again. It's best to keep the point of the chisel pointing towards the centre of the pipe. Try to break it right down to the shoulder of the socket at one point and the rest will then come out fairly easily. Repeat the chipping process to remove all the old jointing material. Remove the bundle of rags or newspaper with the fragments of pipe and jointing material. Then with your cold chisel, remove every trace of the cement base that secured the old pan to the floor.

Installing the new pan

Don't set the pan on a cement base – just use screws and plugs to fix it to the floor. But first you've got to get the connection to the pipe socket right. Start by positioning the patent push-fit joint in the pipe end. Then offer up the new pan to the patent push-fit socket and move the pan around until it fits snugly. To fix the pan, mark the screw positions on the floor by tapping a nail through the screw-holes, and draw round the base on the floor so that you can replace it in exactly the same position. Drill holes in the floor at the points marked and finally fit the screws. If it's a solid floor, of course, it's essential to use plastic or fibre plugs in the screw holes.

For fixing the pan, it's advisable to use brass non-corroding screws with a lead washer slipped over each one so you won't crack the pan as you tighten the screws. Screw the pan down, checking that it is exactly horizontal with the aid of a spirit level laid across the top of the bowl. If it is not dead-level, pack the lower side with thin wood or plastic strips. The latter are more suitable because thin wood rots too easily. Finally check that the outlet of the pan is firmly pushed into the connector and that you've followed any specific fitting instructions from the manufacturer.

Fitting the cistern

Fix the new cistern to the wall at the level above the pan recommended by the manufacturer. In the case of a separate cistern, secure the upper end of the flush pipe to the cistern, usually by means of a large nut, and the lower end to the pan's flushing horn with a rubber cone connector. With a close-coupled suite, follow the manufacturer's instructions. You will now quite likely have to extend or cut back the water supply pipe to connect it to the new cistern. Complete the job by cutting and fitting a new overflow.

INSTALLING A SHOWER

Showers have become a part of the modern home, whether fitted over the bath or in a separate cubicle. They save time, space and energy and are quite easy to install once the design is right.

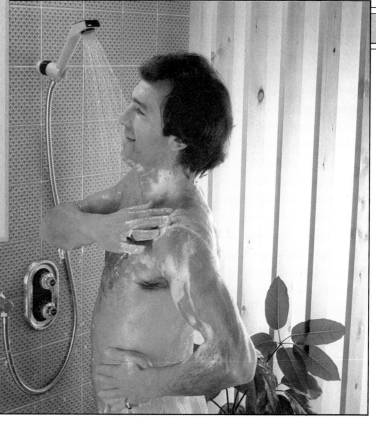

It is possible for four or five members of a family to have showers in the same time – and with the same amount of hot water – that would be needed for just one of them to have a bath. Showers, if properly installed, are safer for use by the elderly and the very young than a sit-down bath and need less cleaning. They are also more hygienic to use than a bath, as the bather isn't sitting in his own soapy and dirty water, and can rinse thoroughly in fresh water.

Where a shower is provided in its own cubicle, as distinct from over a bath, it takes up very little extra space. One can be provided in any space which is at least 900mm (36in) square, and can be put in a variety of locations such as a bedroom, on a landing, in a lobby or even in the cupboard under the stairs.

Yet shower installation can all too often prove to be a disappointment. Poorly designed systems may provide only a trickle of water at the sprinkler, or may run icy cold until the cold tap is almost turned off, and will then run scalding hot.

So, although it is possible to provide a shower in virtually any household, it is important that you match the shower equipment and your existing hot and cold water systems. If you have a cylinder storage hot water system, which is by far the commonest kind of hot water supply to be found in British homes, a conventional shower connected to the household's hot and cold water supplies is likely to be the most satisfactory and the easiest to install. But the hot and cold water systems must comply with certain quite definite design requirements if the shower is to operate safely and satisfactorily.

Pressure

The most important requirement is that the hot and cold supply pipes to the shower must be under equal water pressure. With a cylinder storage hot water system, whether direct or indirect (described on pages 9 to 13), hot water pressure comes from the main cold water storage cistern supplying the cylinder with water. The cold water supply to the shower must therefore also come from

this cistern (or perhaps from a separate cistern at the same level); it must not be taken direct from the cold water main. It is, in fact, illegal to mix, in any plumbing appliance, water which comes direct from the main and water coming from a storage cistern. However, quite apart from the question of legality, it is impossible to mix streams of water satisfactorily under such differing pressures. The shower will inevitably run either very hot or very cold, depending on which stream is the high-pressure one.

The cold water storage cistern must also be high enough above the shower sprinkler to provide a satisfactory operating pressure. Best results will be obtained if the base of the cold water storage cistern is 1.5m (5ft) or more above the sprinkler. However, provided that pipe runs are short and have only slight changes of direction, a reasonable shower can be obtained when the vertical distance between the base of the cistern and the shower sprinkler is as little as 1m (39in). The level of the hot water storage tank in relation to the shower doesn't matter in the least. It can be above, below or at the same level as the shower. It is the level of the cold water storage cistern that matters.

There is yet another design requirement for conventional shower installation which sometimes applies. This is that the cold water supply to the shower should be a separate 15mm (½in) branch direct from the cold water storage cistern, and not taken from the main bathroom distribution pipe. This is a safety precaution. If the cold supply were

taken as a branch from a main distribution pipe, then flushing a lavatory cistern would reduce the pressure on the cold side of the shower causing it to run dangerously hot. For the same reason it is best for the hot supply to be taken direct from the vent pipe immediately above the hot water storage cylinder and not as a branch from another distribution pipe, though this is rather less important. A reduction in the hot water pressure would result in the shower running cold. This would be highly unpleasant, although not dangerous.

Mixers

Showers must have some kind of mixing valve to mix the streams of hot and cold water and thus to produce a shower at the required temperature. The two handles of the bath taps provide the very simplest mixing valve, and push-on shower attachments can be cheaply obtained. Opening the bath taps then mixes the two streams of water and diverts them upwards to a wall-hung shower rose. These very simple attachments work quite satisfactorily – provided that the design requirements already referred to are met. However, it isn't always easy to adjust the tap handles to provide water at exactly the temperature required.

A bath/shower mixer provides a slightly more sophisticated alternative operating on the same principle. With one of these, the tap handles are adjusted until water is flowing through the mixer spout into the bath at the required temperature. The water is then

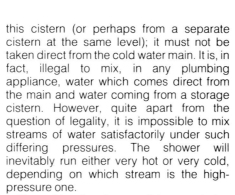

CHOOSING THE RIGHT SHOWER TYPE

The type of shower you can install depends on the sort of water supply you have in your home. This chart will help you make the right selection.

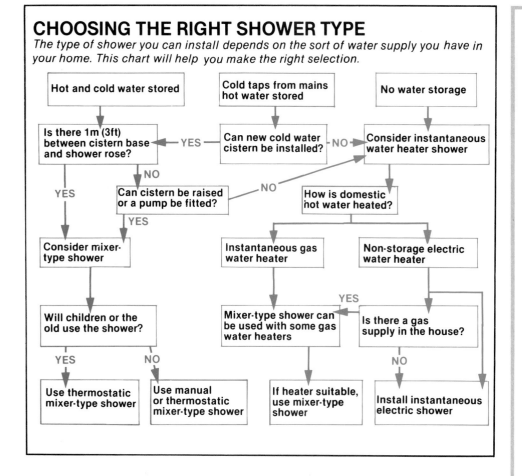

Ready Reference

WHY HAVE A SHOWER?

Showers have many advantages over baths:
● they are hygienic as you don't sit in dirty, soapy water and you get continually rinsed
● they are pleasant to use. Standing under jets of water can be immensely stimulating, especially first thing in the morning
● they use a lot less water per 'wash' than a bath, which saves energy and is also an advantage where water softeners are in use
● economy of hot water usage means that at peak traffic times there is more water to go round
● showers take less time, they don't have to be 'run', and users can't lay back and bask, monopolizing the bathroom
● easy temperature adjustment of a shower gives greater comfort for the user and lessens the risk of catching cold in a cold bathroom.

SHOWER LOCATION

You don't have to install a shower over a bath or even in the bathroom. A bedroom is one alternative site, but landings and utility rooms are another possibility. Provided a supply of water is available, the pressure head satisfactory, and the disposal of waste water possible, a shower can provide a compact and very useful house improvement in many parts of the home.

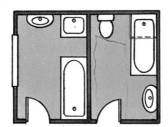

In a bathroom a shower will usually go over a bath, which is the easiest and most popular position. In a larger bathroom a cubicle is a good idea.

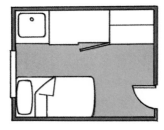

In a bedroom a shower can be easily fitted at the end of built-in wardrobes.

diverted up to the head by turning a valve.

Then there are manual shower mixers. These are standard equipment in independent shower cubicles and may also be used over a bath. With a manual mixer the hot and cold streams of water are mixed in a single valve. Temperature, and sometimes flow control, are obtained by turning large knurled control knobs.

Finally, there are thermostatic shower mixing valves. These may resemble manual mixers in appearance but are designed to accommodate small pressure fluctuations in either the hot or cold water supplies to the shower. They are thus very useful safety devices. But thermostatic valves cannot, even if it were legal, compensate for the very great difference of pressure between mains supply and a supply from a cold water storage cistern. Nor can they add pressure to either the hot or cold supply. If pressure falls on one side of the valve the thermostatic device will reduce flow on the other side to match it.

Thermostatic valves are more expensive but they eliminate the need to take an independent cold water supply pipe from the storage cistern to the shower and can possibly reduce the total cost of installation.

Where a shower is provided over an existing bath, steps must be taken to protect the bathroom floor from splashed water. A plastic shower curtain provides the cheapest means of doing this but a folding, glass shower screen has a much more attractive appearance and is more effective.

Electric showers

You can run your shower independently of the existing domestic hot water system by fitting an instantaneously heated electric one. There are a number of these on the market nowadays. They need only to be connected to the rising main and to a suitable source of electricity to provide an 'instant shower'. You'll find more information about these on pages 115 to 119.

Installing a bath/shower mixer

To install a shower above a bath, first disconnect the water supply, and drain the cistern (see pages 49 to 51). Remove the bath panel, if there is one, and disconnect the tap tails from the supply pipes. Then unscrew and remove the tap back-nuts and take the taps off.

You can now fix the new mixer in place (see pages 106 to 110). Finally, decide on the position for the shower spray bracket and fix it in place.

HOW TO ADAPT YOUR SYSTEM

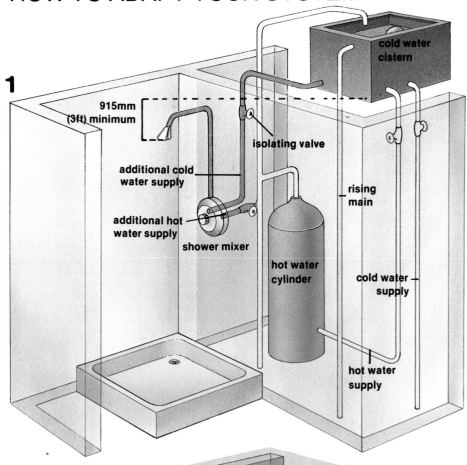

1

915mm
(3ft) minimum

isolating valve

additional cold
water supply

additional hot
water supply

shower mixer

hot water
cylinder

cold water
cistern

rising
main

cold water
supply

hot water
supply

3

flat roof

additional cold
water supply

additional hot
water supply

cold water
cistern

pump

1 : Just add pipework

◁ The most common domestic plumbing system has a cold water cistern in the loft which feeds a hot water tank. In this case you must check that the vertical distance from the bottom of the cold cistern to the shower outlet head is at least 915mm (3ft). To install a shower you must take a 15mm cold water supply direct from the cistern to the cold inlet of the mixer, and a 15mm (1/2in) hot water supply from the draw-off pipe, which emerges from the hot water tank, to the hot water inlet of the mixer.

2 : Raise the cistern

▷ In many older houses the cold water cistern may be in the airing cupboard immediately above the hot water tank, or in another position but still beneath ceiling height. This will usually mean that there is insufficient pressure for a mixer-type shower on the same floor. To get round this problem the cistern can be raised into the loft by extending the pipework upwards. Moving an old galvanised cistern will be rather arduous so this is a good opportunity to replace it with a modern plastic one, (see pages 156 to 159).

3 : Install a pump

◁ In some homes which have flat roofs it is impossible to raise the cistern indoors to provide a sufficient pressure head for a shower on the same floor. While you could consider putting the cistern on top of the roof this would involve providing extensive insulation and is an unsatisfactory solution. Pump-assisted mixer showers are available which will artificially increase the pressure head when the shower is turned on and these are fairly simple to install. As they are electrically operated they should be situated outside the bathroom area.

4 : Add a new cistern

▷ Many modern houses have combination hot and cold water storage units which are supplied and installed as one unit. They have a disadvantage in that cold water capacity is about one-third of the hot water cylinder and would provide an insufficient supply for a shower. This problem can be overcome by installing a pump and a supplementary cold water storage cistern. To ensure similar hot and cold pressures at the shower the supplementary cistern must be at a comparable level with the combination unit's cold water storage.

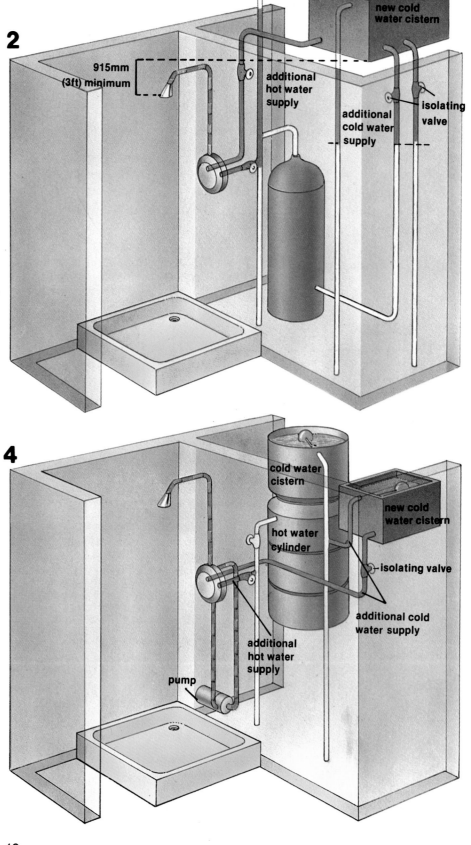

2

915mm (3ft) minimum

additional hot water supply

new cold water cistern

additional cold water supply

isolating valve

4

cold water cistern

hot water cylinder

new cold water cistern

isolating valve

additional cold water supply

additional hot water supply

pump

Ready Reference

TYPES OF SHOWER
There are two basic types of shower:
● those attached to a mixer on a bath
● those independent of the bath, discharging over their own bases, in their own cubicles.

Bath showers may be attached to a mixer head on which you have to adjust both taps, or they may simply fit over the tap outlets. The shower head in either case is detachable and may be mounted at whatever height you require.

Independent showers have fixed position heads or are adjustable. They may have a single control mixer, or a dual control which means that you can adjust the flow as well as the temperature. Thermostatic mixing valves are also available which can cope with small pressure fluctuations in the hot and cold water supply. These only reduce pressure on one side of the valve if that on the other side falls; they cannot increase the pressure unless they have already decreased it.

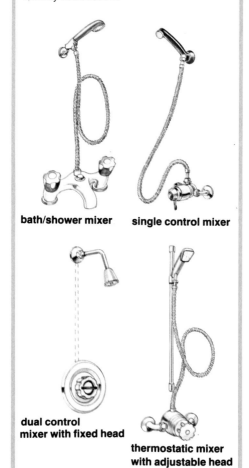

bath/shower mixer   **single control mixer**

dual control mixer with fixed head

thermostatic mixer with adjustable head

PLUMBING IN AN ELECTRIC SHOWER

If you would like to install a shower but think you can't because there's insufficient water pressure, you might like to consider an instantaneous electric shower. It's connected directly to the mains cold water supply, so you are guaranteed a good jet of water. And as you heat only the water you use, it's very economical to run.

U ntil quite recently a properly functioning shower was all but an impossibility in many homes. Either it lacked the cylinder storage hot water system needed to supply a conventional shower, or the system that existed wouldn't permit a successful shower installation. For example, the main cold water storage cistern might have had insufficient capacity to supply the cold side of the shower mixer as well as feeding the hot water storage cylinder, or it may have been situated at too low a level to give adequate pressure at the shower rose. (For more information about the theory of shower design see previous section.)

The increasing popularity of showers has led to two new developments: the electric shower pump which increases pressure at the shower rose where this is inadequate; and the instantaneous electric shower.

Going back to geysers

There is nothing particularly new about appliances which heat water 'instantaneously' as it flows through them. The Edwardian geyser, installed over the bath in many a turn-of-the century middle-class home, was an early example. The modern single-point or multi-point instantaneous gas water heater – which can provide hot water for the whole house – is its direct descendant. Instantaneous water heaters were designed for connection directly to the rising main so they could operate under mains pressure. They needed no cold water storage cistern or storage cylinder and they had the advantage that heat energy was expended only to heat water that was actually to be used at that time.

However, until a couple of decades ago, the only instantaneous water heating appliances that were available were – like the early geysers – gas-operated. It just wasn't possible to devise an electric appliance that could 'instantaneously' heat a sufficiently large volume of water to fill a sit-down bath, a sink or even a wash basin. It still isn't. But

manufacturers have now produced electric water heaters powerful enough to provide a steady flow of hot water for spray hand-washing over a washbasin in a WC compartment and for the provision of a shower. In neither case is very hot water needed in large volumes.

An instantaneous electric water heater is a relatively compact appliance that needs only to be connected – by means of a 15mm (½in) branch water supply pipe – to the main supply, and to a suitable supply of electricity. It is normally operated by a flow-switch which ensures that electricity is switched on only when water is flowing through the appliance. As it does so, it passes over powerful electrical heating elements.

Temperature control was originally obtained solely by controlling the volume of water flowing through the heater. Opening up the tap or control valve produced a heavy flow of cool water. As the control valve was closed down and the flow diminished, warmer and warmer water was obtained from the shower spray.

The crude, early models were something of a disaster and were frowned on by water authorities and electricity boards. They rarely provided a satisfactory shower. The flow was markedly less than that from a conventional, cylinder-supplied shower. Flushing the WC or opening up any other tap in the house would reduce the pressure of the water entering the heater, so reducing the flow and raising the water temperature from the shower spray. Such unpredictable temperature changes could cause serious scalding to an unsuspecting user. Other problems arose from the hard water scale that tended to form on the heating elements.

Instantaneous showers today

However, an unhappy experience a decade or so ago with one of the early instantaneous electric showers need not deter you from having a modern one installed today. There have been some tremendous advances in design and construction and you can be confident that a modern model will work

WHAT'S INSIDE THE CASING

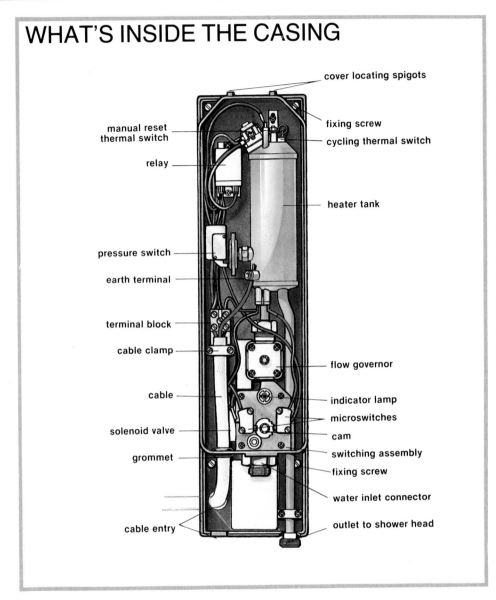

cover locating spigots

manual reset thermal switch

fixing screw

cycling thermal switch

relay

heater tank

pressure switch

earth terminal

terminal block

cable clamp

flow governor

cable

indicator lamp

microswitches

solenoid valve

cam

switching assembly

grommet

fixing screw

water inlet connector

cable entry

outlet to shower head

properly provided that it is properly installed according to the manufacturer's instructions.

Most instantaneous showers must be supplied with water at a minimum pressure of 1.05kg per sq cm (15lb per sq in). They are intended for connection direct to the mains supply, though they can be supplied by a cistern if it is at least 10.75m (35ft) above the level of the shower spray. In most cases mains water pressure will be adequate, but those who live in an area where mains pressure is low should check the actual pressure with their local water authority before incurring the expense of installation.

Modern electric showers usually have an electrical loading of 6kW to 7kW and it is often possible, for the sake of economy, to switch to a low setting of 3kW or 4kW during the summer months. Choose a model that incorporates a temperature stabiliser. This is an anti-scald device that maintains the water

temperature at the level chosen by the user of the shower, despite any fluctuations in pressure which may result from water being drawn off from taps or by flushing the W.C. Should there be a drop in pressure beyond the capacity of the stabiliser, a safety sensor turns the shower off completely.

When choosing your instantaneous electric shower, look for evidence that it has been approved by such national safety committees as the B.E.A.B., the National Water Council and the A.N.T. (Assessment of Techniques) Committee of the Institute of Electrical Engineers.

Fitting a shower

Although instantaneous electric showers can be fitted over a sit-down bath, they are usually installed in a separate shower cubicle which may be in a bathroom, in a bedroom or even on a landing. The shower tray must

have a trapped outlet and the branch waste pipe can discharge by the same route as basin or bath wastes (see WASTE WATER SYSTEMS, pages 14 to 18).

Plumbing connections should be straightforward. It's best to connect the supply pipe to the shower heater first and then work backwards to the main supply, making this connection last of all. In this way you will interrupt the supply to the rest of the house as little as possible.

The connection to the shower may be a simple compression coupling (described on pages 20 to 24) or it may have a screwed male thread. In which case you'll need a compression fitting with a coupling at one end and a female screwed connector at the other. To connect into the rising main you should use a compression tee (as described on pages 28 to 32).

Obtaining the power

Instantaneous showers get their power from a separate radial circuit taken from the consumer unit. As most models of shower have a loading of either 6 or 7kW they can be supplied safely by a circuit that has a current rating of 30A and is run in 6mm^2 two-core and earth cable. Recently, however, an 8kW shower has been introduced on the market by some manufacturers. This shouldn't pose extra problems for anyone intending to install it: provided the radial circuit originates at either a cartridge fuse or MCB – which both have the effect of uprating the circuit by one third – then a 30A circuit will be adequate to install. Should you decide to install one of these larger showers then it's still probably a good idea to check their requirements with the makers beforehand.

Showers should be controlled by a 30A double-pole cord-operated switch. From this a length of 6mm^2 two-core and earth cable will run to the shower unit. There is one type that requires a slightly different method of connecting up. If you're going to fit a shower that has a control unit already connected to a length of three-core flex then you'll have to fix a flex outlet unit on the wall near the shower unit so you can connect the flex into the circuit.

Fitting the switch

Ceiling switches can either be surface or flush mounted. If you're going to surface mount one, you'll have to pierce a hole in the ceiling so the cables can be drawn through into a plastic mounting box. Before fixing this in position with No 8 wood screws, you should knock a thin section of plastic from the base to align with the hole in the ceiling. Ideally the box should be fitted against a joist, but if there isn't one suitably placed, you'll have to fix a support batten between the joists made from 75 x 25mm (3 x 1in) timber with a hole drilled in it big enough to let two lengths of

INSTALLING THE SHOWER UNIT

1 First take the shower spray support assembly and fix it to the wall. It is important to follow the manufacturer's recommendations as to height.

2 Remove the control knobs and any other fittings from the shower unit to enable the faceplate to be taken off before further installation takes place.

3 Carefully position the unit on the shower cubicle wall and mark the screw fitting holes, water and power channels; drill out the fixing holes.

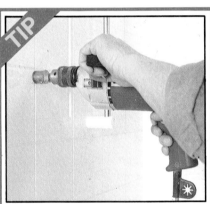

4 Using a hole saw attachment for your drill, cut holes in the cubicle wall for the water and power supplies, then fix the unit to the wall.

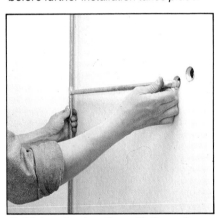

5 Make a tee junction with the main, and run a length of pipe to the water access; then add an elbow and length of pipe to go through the wall.

6 Use a swivel tap connector to attach the cold water feed to the unit; this is linked to the inlet pipe by a soldered capillary joint.

7 Make sure the fibre washer in the connector is in place; then screw it up and tighten. Don't use any sealant on the nylon inlet.

8 Attach the shower hose to the screwed outlet, making sure that the rubber washer is in place. Then make the electrical connections (page 118).

9 Turn on the water supply and also the electricity to make sure that the unit works. Finally, replace the cover and control knobs.

6mm² cable pass through. When you're feeding the cables into the mounting box, it's a good idea to write 'mains' on the end of the circuit cable and 'shower' on the end of the shower feed cable. This could be surface mounted on the ceiling and wall, but it's neater to conceal it in the ceiling void and chase it into the wall, running it in plastic conduit.

You can now strip back the insulation and make the connections. The mains cable should go to the 'supply' side of the switch, with the red core going to the terminal marked L and the black to the one marked N, and the shower cable to the equivalent terminals on the 'load' side. Remember to sleeve the earth cores in green/yellow PVC and connect them to the earth terminal in the switch. Place the six cores neatly in the box and screw the switch to it.

If you're going to flush-mount the switch you'll have to mark the size of the mounting box on the ceiling and, using a pad saw, carefully cut out an equivalent size hole. Then cut a piece of timber to fit between the joists, lay it across the hole and mark the square on it. Knock out a blank from the base of the metal box and drill a hole in the corresponding spot in the timber. Then screw the box to the timber and fix the timber to the joists at a height above the ceiling that allows the box edge to sit flush with the ceiling surface. This can be checked by holding a straight edge across the hole in the ceiling. You should then thread in the two marked cables and make the connections. If you want to fix the switch at a point where there is a joist you can always cut away a section of it. This is best done by using a drill fitted with a 25mm (1in) wood bit to remove most of the wood and then chiselling the remainder away. That way you won't need access to the ceiling void as long as you can 'fish' the cable across the ceiling using a length of stiff wire.

Connecting into the shower

The cable to the shower can be run down the wall on the surface, using plastic cable clips or mini-trunking, or buried in a chase chopped in the plaster. The cover of the control unit must be removed to allow you access to the terminal block, but do read fully the manufacturer's instructions before going any further. Thread in the cable and strip off some of the sheathing and insulation before connecting the red core to the L terminal and the black to the N terminal. Before connecting the earth core to the earth terminal make sure you've sleeved it in green/yellow PVC. If the unit has a cable clamp, fix the cable in it, double checking that it's the whole, sheathed cable that is held by it and not just individual cores. This is very important as it serves to protect the con-

CONNECTING THE POWER

1 After fixing the shower unit to the bathroom wall and making the connection from the rising main, thread in the circuit cable.

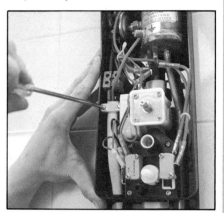

2 Feed the cable up the unit and strip it before connecting the red and black cores to the L and N terminals respectively.

3 Remember to sleeve the bare earth core in green/yellow PVC before feeding it into the earth terminal and connecting it up.

4 Then make sure that the clamp plate will bear down on the cable sheathing before tightening it up to protect all the connections.

nections. Finally, refit the unit cover, finish off the radial circuit connections at the consumer unit, switch on at the mains and test the shower.

Fitting a flex outlet plate

You'll have to use a flex outlet plate only if there is already a flex connected to the shower unit. This can be fitted on either a one-gang moulded plastic box for surface mounting, or else in a 35mm (1½in) metal box for flush mounting, in which case you'll have to chop a hole. After fixing one or other of the boxes to the wall, run the cable into it through a knockout hole, which, in the case of the metal box, should be fitted with a grommet. The unit has three banks of terminals with two terminal screws per bank and you should connect the green/yellow sleeved earth core to a terminal of the non-shielded bank marked 'E'. Then connect the red insulated core to a terminal of one of the shielded banks and the black to a terminal of the other bank.

Prepare the end of the flex by stripping off approximately 12mm (½in) of insulation from the end of each core. Remember to thread the flex through the hole in the unit's cover before you connect the flex to the unit as you won't be able to fit it after you've made the connections. Then connect the earth core, which should be already sleeved in green and yellow PVC, to the other terminal in the 'E' bank, the brown core to the bank containing the red core and the blue core to the bank containing the black circuit core. Tighten the cord clamp, again making sure that it's the flex sheath that it grips and not the unsheathed cores as this protects the connections. Lay the six cores neatly in the box and fix the unit to the box with the two screws supplied. You can then switch on the power and test the shower.

THE ELECTRICAL CONNECTIONS

— 6mm² cable

30A DP ceiling switch

power supply

to shower

Providing and controlling the power to an instantaneous shower is straightforward and making the connections is quite simple.

1 The ceiling switch: *feed in the two cables and mark the power supply cable 'mains' and the shower cable 'shower'. Connect the cores of the power cable to the terminals on the supply side and the shower cable to the load side of the switch.*

shower unit

2 The terminal block: *feed the cable under the clamp and connect the red core to L, the black core to N and the green/yellow PVC sleeved earth core to the earth screw on the heater tank. Make sure you tighten the clamp on the cable and not individual cores.*

FITTING A CEILING SWITCH

power supply
to shower
joist
surface box
30A DP ceiling switch
timber batten

power supply
to shower
joist
30A DP ceiling switch
timber batten
one gang metal box

Surface mounted: *try to mount the switch on a joist. If you can't, fit a timber batten. Drill holes in the batten and ceiling to admit the cables and remove a knockout from the base of the box. Fix the box to the ceiling and make the connections.*

Flush mounted: *use a pad saw to cut a hole in the ceiling for the mounting box. Fix the box to a batten between the joists and set the batten so the box is flush with the ceiling. Feed the cables through and make the connections.*

Ready Reference

PLUMBING REQUIREMENTS
The shower unit should be connected directly to the cold water mains supply. If this isn't possible, a storage tank may be used to supply the unit; but it must be about 10.75m (35ft) above the shower spray head.

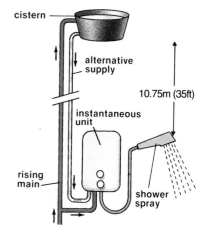

cistern
alternative supply
10.75m (35ft)
instantaneous unit
rising main
shower spray

USING THE SHOWER
After turning on the unit, you'll have to wait a short while so the water retained in the heater tank and shower fittings from the last shower is drawn off. The water temperature is controlled by the rate of flow through the heater – the slower the flow rate, the higher the temperature, and vice versa. Because the cold water supply is likely to be comparatively colder in the winter than in summer, this means in winter you may have to put up with a slower flow rate in order to get the required temperature.

ELECTRICAL CONNECTION
When you're wiring up an instantaneous shower, you must ensure that:
● it is permanently connected to its own separate 30A power supply, and is properly earthed
● it is controlled by a 30A double-pole cord-operated switch mounted on the ceiling. An ordinary ceiling light switch is not suitable.

NEVER turn on the electricity supply until all the plumbing has been completed, including mounting the handset and hose, and the power supply and earthing connections are made.

CONNECTING SHOWER FITTINGS

Before you get to grips with installing a new shower cubicle, you ought to select the type of control fitting you're going to use. Your choice may affect the way you organise the plumbing.

Once you've decided where you're going to site your shower – over a bath or in a separate cubicle – you'll have to determine what type of fitting you're going to use to run it. In order for the shower to work effectively, you need to be able to control the rate of flow of water and also, more importantly, it's temperature. There's nothing worse than standing under a stuttering supply of water that's hot one minute and cold the next. So it's the job of the shower fitting to provide this control fast and effectively.

Some fittings work by having individual taps to control the hot and cold water supplies, while the more sophisticated types have a simple valve or a mixer. How they are connected up to the water supply depends primarily on their design. For example, instantaneous showers (see the previous section) need only to be connected to the mains cold water supply, as they heat all the hot water required just before it comes out of the shower rose. A hot water supply is therefore unnecessary. But for all other showers, the temperature of the water is controlled by mixing together separate supplies of hot and cold water which may also be at different pressures.

The simplest fittings

Before proper showers over a bath and separate shower cubicles became popular, it was quite common to find a rather makeshift device being used to supply a spray of water. This consisted of a length of rubber hose with a rose attached at one end and two connectors fitted at the other which slipped over the hot and cold taps on the bath. By adjusting these taps you could regulate the flow and temperature of the water. In fact the principle of this very basic mixing valve was used in early shower cubicles. Gate valves on the hot and cold distribution pipes were used to control the flow, and the two supplies were mixed at a 'tee' in the pipework before being fed in a single pipe to an overhead shower rose.

Mixer taps

An improvement on this very simple arrangement, as far as showers over baths are concerned, is the bath/shower mixer. This resembles an ordinary mixer tap on a bath, except that a flexible metal hose rises from the centre of the mixer to a spray head which can be fixed at varying heights on the wall above the bath. Again the water is mixed by adjusting the hot and cold taps, and at this stage it will be coming out of the spout of the tap. When the required temperature has been reached you pull up a lever on the body of the tap and this diverts the water upwards to the spray head.

Nowadays, showers in cubicles normally have what's known as a manual mixing valve. This has two inlets, one for the hot and another for the cold supply; but the temperature is regulated by turning just one mixer knob. The flow may also be adjusted by turning another knob which is set round the outside of the temperature control. In this way you can control the water more quickly and positively than you could do if you had to adjust two separate taps (which tends to be a bit of a juggling act).

Shower mixers are constantly being improved so that they are more convenient and safer to use. With one modern manual mixing valve, for example, the temperature of the water is controlled by turning a knurled knob, not unlike the handle of a tap. And the flow and on/off control is worked by pushing in or pulling out this knob. You can therefore control the flow and temperature of the water

in one movement. Another advantage of this kind of control is that the shower can be stopped instantly if the pressure on the cold side falls (as a result of a toilet being flushed or cold water being drawn off elsewhere in the house, for example). If this happened the shower would suddenly run very hot, but by flicking the control knob downwards the flow ceases. It's not so serious if the pressure falls on the hot side, because the shower would just run cold. But again, to prevent discomfort the flow can be stopped quickly by flicking the control knob.

However, prevention is better than cure and there are ways of organising the plumbing so that this problem can't arise. To alleviate the danger it's best to run the 15mm (½in) cold water supply pipe to the shower direct from the cold water storage cistern and not as a branch from the 22mm (¾in) distribution pipe to the bathroom. This will supply a continuous volume of cold water provided the cistern is working properly.

Thermostatic valves

Of course it may mean too much of an upheaval to lay in a new pipe run, but instead you could install a special thermostatic mixing valve. This enables you to pre-set the temperature of the shower water and this will remain constant despite fluctuations of pressure in the hot and cold supplies. And apart from this, thermostatic mixers provide

INSTALLING A FIXED ROSE

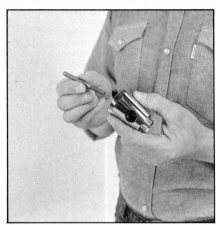

1 To mount the wall fixing, thread one end of the double-ended screw supplied into the hole in the base of the casting.

2 With the flange in place, screw the fitting into the shower wall using a pre-drilled fixing hole. The inlet hole must point downwards.

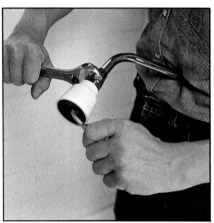

3 Screw the outlet rose onto the outlet pipe by removing the rose and inserting an Allen key into the recess you will find inside.

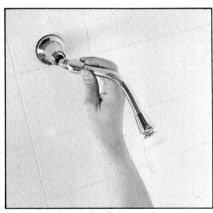

4 Attach the outlet fitting to the wall fixing, by tightening the fixing nut on the rose so it crushes the olive. But don't chip the chrome.

5 Make sure that the outlet rose swivels firmly but freely on its ball bearing, and that it emerges at right angles to the wall.

6 Screw the supply pipe into the outlet supply until it is tight against the washer, and check that it is truly vertical.

7 Attach the supply pipe to the thermostatic control unit and mark the position of the supply pipe holes on the shower wall.

8 Turn off the water supplies via stop-valves, if fitted, and tee off the supply pipes to feed the hot and cold inlets of the shower mixer.

9 Drill holes in the shower wall so that the supply pipes can be fed through from behind and connected up to the shower mixer.

INSTALLING AN ADJUSTABLE ROSE

1 *Fit the two wall fixing brackets to the end of the runner, and align them both so that they are pointing in the same direction.*

2 *Mark the positions for the fixing screws on the shower wall, drill the holes and then proceed to screw on the uppermost bracket.*

3 *Slide on the movable rose support and fix the lower bracket to the wall. Cover the screw entry holes with plastic caps.*

4 *Take the one-piece shower head and rose and screw on the flexible hose, making sure that the fibre washer is correctly placed.*

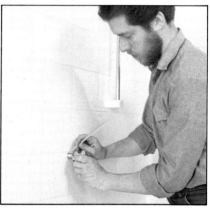

5 *Hold the wall supply point fixing in place and mark the wall for drilling. Drill the hole, making sure you don't damage the tiled surround.*

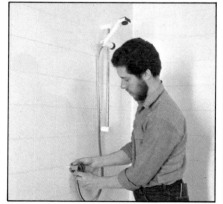

6 *Insert the fixing and screw it up tight. Then take your chosen mixer, drill its fixing holes and plumb in the supply pipes.*

just that extra margin of safety and assurance against discomfort.

Before buying a thermostatic mixing valve, it's important that you recognise its limitations as well as its advantages. These valves can deal with relatively minor fluctuations in pressure that can result from water being drawn off from one or other of the supply pipes. They can't accommodate the great differences in pressure between a hot water supply under pressure from a storage cylinder and a cold supply taken direct from the main (in any case, you should never arrange your shower plumbing in this way). Some thermostatic valves even require a greater working 'hydraulic head' (the vertical distance between the cold water cistern and the shower rose) than the 1m (3ft) minimum that is usual for manual mixers. So it's a good idea to check on these points and on the 'head' available before you buy one of them.

Shower pumps

An inadequate 'head' is, of course, one of the commonest reasons why a shower won't work properly. Although the minimum distance between the base of the cold water cistern and the shower rose must be 1m (3ft), for best results this distance ought to be 1.5m (5ft) or more.

However, all is not lost if you can't get this head because you can install a shower pump. They're expensive but they can make the difference between a stimulating shower and a miserable, low-pressure trickle, which isn't much good to anyone.

Different types of pump are controlled in different ways. Some have manual switches which are controlled by a pull-cord. In this case the pump is only switched on after the water has begun to flow, and is turned off before it has been stopped. Other pumps are operated automatically when the water is

turned on at the shower by the movement of water in the pipes.

You can install a simple pump between the mixer and the shower rose outlet, but you may find it difficult to conceal. On the other hand, automatic pumps must be connected into the water supply before it reaches the mixer, so it's easier to choose a convenient site where the pump can be hidden from view or disguised.

Shower pumps need quite a lot of plumbing in, and if you're not careful about planning you may end up with a lot of exposed pipework. It's also worth remembering that when you wire up the electricity supply you have to connect the pump to a fused connection unit with a double-pole switch. And if the pump is situated inside the bathroom it must be protected from steam and water (except in the case of units specially designed to be inside the shower cubicle).

THREE TYPES OF SHOWER

There are several types of shower mixer available on the market. They fall into two types – those which simply mix the hot and cold flows, and those which make an effort to provide the mixed flows at a constant, pre-set, temperature. All of them are usually finished in chrome and the controls are made of a strong plastic which will resist most knocks and blows.

Surface-mounted mixer
Left: This is a surface-mounted mixer control with separate supply pipes emerging through the wall to supply the control which provides power over flow and temperature.

Built-in mixer
Right: This built-in control is supplied from behind the shower wall so that the supply pipes are hidden. These fittings are also available in a gold finish.

Thermostatic mixer
Left: This thermostatic mixer is also supplied from behind and provides two separate controls – one for pre-setting the temperature, and one for adjusting the flow of the water once the user is inside the shower.

Ready Reference

TYPES OF SUPPLY

Here is a summary of the various types of shower supply you could choose:

Rear supply – surface mounting
Both hot and cold supplies come through the wall behind the mixer, which is surface mounted on the cubicle wall.

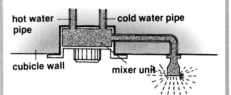

Surface supply – surface mixing
The hot and cold supplies come independently through the shower wall and can be seen entering the surface-mounted mixing unit.

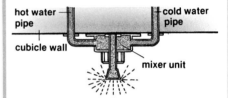

Surface supply – thermostatic mixing
Water supplies come through the wall into the surface-mounted unit, and then are regulated by sensitive flow and temperature controls.

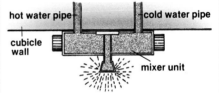

Rear supply – instantaneous shower
The mains (cold-water only) supply comes through or along the wall, and enters the unit for rapid heating and distribution through the rose.

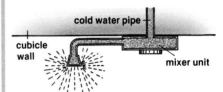

TIP: TEST YOUR SEALS

However much purpose-built shower surround you buy – or however much you build – it must all have a waterproof seal with the tray and any solid cubicle walls. Test all joints for leaks with a hand spray, and if they do leak, make sure they are filled with a flexible non-setting mastic.

BUILDING A SHOWER CUBICLE

The simplest way to add showering facilities to your bathroom is to install the shower over the bath. However, building a separate cubicle is a better solution.

When you come to install a shower in your home, the most obvious place for it is over the bath because you can make use of the bath's water supply and waste facilities. But this isn't the most advantageous site: putting a shower there does not increase your bathing facilities, it merely improves the existing ones. It's far better to have your shower as a separate cubicle, even if the cubicle is in the bathroom itself. If you can put the cubicle in another part of the home, you have as good as provided an extra bathroom.

You may think that you have no room in your home for a shower outside the bathroom, but that is not necessarily true. A shower does not require all that much space and you can make do with an area about 900mm (3ft) square. But you've got to think about how much space you need to get into and out of the shower. It isn't usually that easy or efficient to dry off inside, so you need some space to dry off at the point of exit. You will also have to take into consideration the relationship of the drying area with bathroom fittings.

You can buy a ready-made shower cubicle, or build your own from scratch. The latter course will save a lot of money, and is easier than you might think, but you've got to take care to ensure that it is properly waterproofed.

Putting in the tray
To build a shower cubicle you start with the shower tray. Many people attempt to make one of these themselves by building a box that they cover with some impervious material – usually tiles. However, the construction is not easy because making the box absolutely waterproof can present problems, and then it is difficult to get the right gradient from every part of the tray to carry water to the waste outlet. On the whole, you would do better to buy a tray.

Normally, trays are made in acrylic plastic or glazed ceramics. The latter are dearer, but much longer-lasting, as acrylics can crack. Both types are available in standard sanitary-ware colours, so if you have a modern coloured bathroom suite, you should be able to match it. Trays come in a range of sizes, so be sure to choose one to fit

the space you have, since obviously the size of tray governs the area your installation will take up. Ceramic trays can also be very heavy so it's likely you'll need help to get one into position.

The tray will have a waste outlet, and this may be in one corner, or in the middle of one side. It must be sited so that its waste pipe can discharge conveniently into a hopper of a two-pipe system, or be connected up to an existing waste pipe, or to the main stack of a single-pipe system. The waste pipe must slope downwards all the way, and it is important to get the fall right in order to drain water away efficiently. In general, the fall should be between 6 and 50mm per 300mm run of pipe (¼ to 2in per ft) depending on the length of the run (measured from the actual waste outlet). Too steep a run can produce a siphonage effect that will drain the water out of the trap, thus depriving your home of its protection from drain smells (see pages 14 to 18). It's a good idea to set a fall of 25mm (1in) per 300mm for a short run of say 600 to 900mm (2 to 3ft), but only a 12mm (½in) fall where the run will be 3 to 4.5m (10 to 15ft).

Most shower trays are square, and obviously these can be turned round to place the outlet in the most convenient position. However, for installation in a corner, triangular shaped trays, or quadrants – with two straight

sides at right angles and a curved front – are on sale, but they're quite expensive.

The outlet does not have a plug, because it is never the intention that the tray should be filled up. Since there is no plug, no overflow is required. However, like all your bathroom fittings, it must have a trap. This should be 38mm (1½in) in diameter but, like a bath, does not have to be of the deep-seal variety.

Some trays are designed to have enough depth to enable the trap to be installed above floor level. Others are quite shallow, and the trap must go under the floor, a point to bear in mind if you have a concrete floor. Yet another possibility is to mount the tray on supports, to raise its height, and some manufacturers sell special supports to raise the tray off the ground. Otherwise you can use bricks or timber, suitably disguised by a plinth. It's a good idea to provide an inspection panel should you ever want to get access to the plumbing. Whatever the case, you will never have good access to the outlet plumbing after it's been installed – so be sure to make a good job of it.

Providing a cubicle
A shower tray is best positioned in a corner, so that two sides of the shower enclosure are already provided by the shower tray itself; you can bridge the gap with timber covered with tiles set flush with the top of the tray.

INSTALLING THE SHOWER TRAY

1 Press a sausage of plumber's putty around the underside of the outlet flange, then wind PTFE tape along the length of the thread.

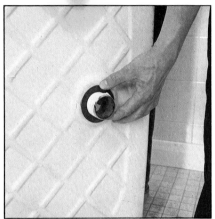

2 Push the flange into the waste hole in the tray, press it home until the putty squeezes out round the edge, and put on the metal washer.

3 Screw on the back-nut by hand and tighten it with an adjustable wrench. This will squeeze more putty out; remove the excess neatly.

4 Take the special low-seal shower trap and screw it onto the outlet flange, after first making sure that the O ring is in place.

5 Measure up the position needed for the waste run, and install the plastic waste pipe in position ready to be connected up to the trap.

6 Lower the tray into place and connect up the trap to the waste pipe. Check that it is level on your prepared base.

Ready Reference

WASTE OUTLET RUNS

You must provide sufficient depth underneath the shower tray to accommodate the waste trap and the outlet pipe. You can:
● support the tray on timber or bricks and face the elevation with panels

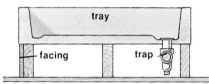

● support the tray with special supporting brackets which are usually available from shower tray manufacturers, and face the elevation with panels

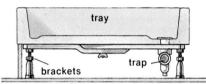

● cut a hole in the floor – if it's made of wood – and run the trap and waste above the ceiling of the room underneath. You can do this only if the joists run in the same direction as the waste pipe.

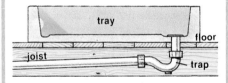

HOW MUCH SPACE?

It's very easy to think of a shower as only occupying the same space as the tray itself. But don't forget that you will usually step out of it soaking wet and so will need sufficient area in which to dry off. If the shower is enclosed on three sides you will need more space than if it's enclosed on one side and curtained on the others.

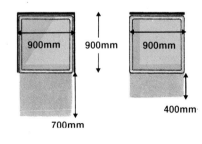

PUTTING UP A SURROUND KIT

1 Mark the position of the wall uprights; use a spirit level to make sure that they will be truly vertical when fixed in position.

2 Drill holes for the upright fixings, then plug them with plastic wall plugs and screw on the uprights with the screws supplied.

3 Slide the first panel into position on the wall upright and fix it; again check that the structure is in a properly vertical position.

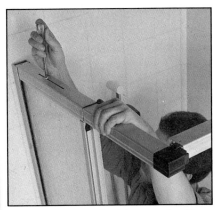

4 Adjust the length of the panel to fit the size of the shower tray and tighten up the screws carefully. Attach the corner bracket.

5 Fix the other panel in position and adjust its length so that it mates up accurately and squarely with the corner bracket.

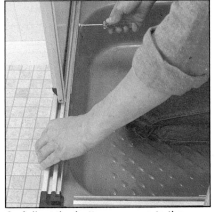

6 Adjust the bottom runners to the correct size so that they match up with the bottom corner bracket; check they are square to the tray.

7 Screw up the bottom corner bracket, then check that the whole structure is firm and square and that the door opens and closes smoothly.

8 Loosen the wall upright fixings and wedge up each side in turn. Squeeze sealant between the frame and the tray and refix the frame.

9 Check again for alignment, then finish off the base by firmly fixing the supports in position and finally boarding in the sides of the shower.

Existing walls forming part of the cubicle will also need tiling or covering with some laminated material – commonly waterproofed decorative wallboard, or even glass or sheet plastic over paint or wallpaper. It is obviously very important to make sure that all gaps are sealed, otherwise gradual water seepage will occur which will damage the fabric of your house.

The sides of the cubicle you have to install can be home-made or bought as kits. The simplest way to fill one or two sides is with a curtain rail and shower curtain. This works quite well with a shower in the bath, but the sides of a shower tray are much shallower than those of a bath and water is therefore quite likely to splash onto the floor. This means that curtains are really only at all suitable for the entry side of the cubicle where you might protect the floor with a bath mat, or where the floor of your bathroom is tiled and fully sealed.

You can construct any solid sides of the cubicle using a timber framework, but you will have to buy a suitable proprietary door unless you use a curtain. These doors are usually made of aluminium frames with opaque safety glass or plastic panels. They come in a wide variety of designs and colours. You can have, for example, a plain aluminium frame with clear glass, or a gold satin frame with dark smoked glass. If you plan to buy a door, check that you have calculated the size of your cubicle to fit it, and that the door comes with suitable rust-proof fittings to hang it.

The easiest (though most expensive) solution is to buy the complete surround, including a sliding or ordinary door, which will be supplied in kit form. These surrounds are made by the same manufacturers as shower doors and usually come complete with fixing instructions. They are usually adjustable to fit different shower tray sizes, and are simply fitted to the wall at each end to provide a rigid frame. Before finishing they have to be sealed where they meet the tray using a proprietary sealant, to ensure a waterproof joint. If this isn't done perfectly, water will gradually seep in and cause damp on the floor and walls of your bathroom.

Home-made surrounds

Making your own surround will save money, and it has the advantage that you can tailor it exactly to your needs. You might, for example, want a surround which is larger than the tray itself; in which case you can install a shelf or seat next to the tray.

Begin by making a framework of 50mm (2in) square timber. You need a length on every edge, plus extra horizontal ones at 450mm (18in) centres. All should be joined with halving joints. In addition, fit any extra length needed to provide a fixing point (for

the shower rose, for instance). The inside face of the partition should then be clad with 6mm (¼in) plywood. Use an exterior-grade board if the cubicle is to be tiled.

Another possibility is to use 10mm (⅜in) thick plasterboard. The framework for this should consist of a 50mm (2in) square batten on every edge, plus one extra vertical and horizontal in the middle, and any additional member needed to provide a fixing point. Fix the board with galvanised plasterboard nails driven in until the head slightly dimples the surface of the board, but without fracturing the paper liner. You can use 3mm (⅛in) hardboard to cover the outside of the cubicle framework.

Do not fix the exterior cladding for the time being. You should first clad the inside face, then fix the half-completed partition in place by driving screws through the frame members into the floor below, the wall behind and the ceiling too if it is to be a room height job.

The interior of this partition is a good place in which to conceal the supply pipes to the shower. You would then need an inspection panel, held by screws (not glued and nailed) to allow easy access to the pipework should maintenance ever be needed.

If the cubicle is not a floor-to-ceiling one, you will also need extra support at the top as you cannot leave the front top edge flapping free. This can take the form of a 75x25mm (3x1in) batten, decoratively moulded if you wish, spanning the two sides of the cubicle or fixed at one end to a block screwed to the wall, should there be only one side.

The whole interior of the shower cubicle needs to be clad with an impervious material to make sure it is waterproof. The most obvious choice is tiles, and these can be fixed to both the plywood or plasterboard cladding and the plaster of a wall. Make sure that the latter is clean and sound before tiling. Do not, however, fix the tiles direct to the timber part of the framing.

As an alternative to tiles you could use a special plastic-faced hardboard, with a tile pattern and a backing of plain hardboard. Fix the plastic-faced board by glueing and pinning with rustproof nails (if these can be lost somewhere in the pattern). Otherwise use a contact adhesive. This does not need to be spread all over the meeting surfaces. Apply it in a pattern similar to that detailed for the framework of the partitions. Adhesives applied by gun are available for this sort of work. The board on the back wall should be fixed in a similar manner.

Whatever material you use, all joins – where partitions meet the wall, or the tray – should be sealed with a silicone bath sealant. Any parts not clad with impervious material should be well painted with a three-coat system of primer, undercoat and one or two top coats.

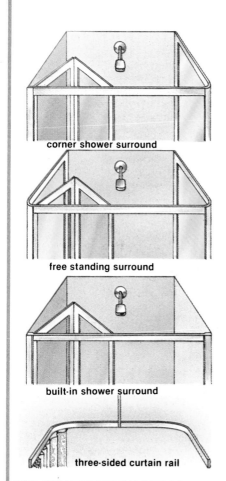
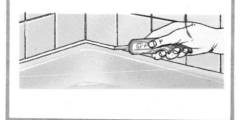

OUTSIDE TAPS AND PIPES

It's vital to know where your main water supply pipes are buried, so you don't damage them by accident and can trace a leak if one occurs. And it's useful to be able to install an outside tap.

Apart from any outside pipes you have, say, supplying a garden tap, the pipe you have to worry about is the service pipe which runs as a branch from the authority's main to supply your house's plumbing system. Usually it will run in a straight line from the authority's stop-valve to the point at which it enters the house and rises through the floor (usually in the kitchen) to become the rising main (see pages 9 to 13).

Because the service pipe is probably the most important water pipe in the home, it's vital that you know where the authority's stop-valve – which controls the flow of water in the pipe – is located. Often you'll find it under a small square or round hinged metal cover set in the pavement just outside the front gate, or in the concrete of your front garden path. It's quite likely that the valve will be protected in a guard pipe beyond the reach of a groping hand. It may have an ordinary crutch handle (the type found on old-fashioned taps) or a specially-shaped square head that can be turned only with one of the water authority's turnkeys.

Provided that you have another 'householder's stop-valve' where the service pipe enters your home, you will rarely have occasion to turn off the authority's stop-valve, but it's nice to be able to feel that you can do so should the need arise. Long-handled keys are available for turning crutch handles, or you may be able to improvise one by cutting a notch in the end of a piece of 75mm x 25mm (3in x 1in) timber and nailing another piece of wood across the other end to serve as a handle. You may have difficulty getting hold of a turnkey for the square-headed type of valve, as the water authority likes to feel that it can turn it off in the event of non-payment of the water rate, without the prospect of it being promptly turned on again, but they are usually entrusted to plumbers in whom the authority has confidence. It's really worth checking out what sort of tap you have, and if you find you haven't got a stop-valve on the rising main inside, you should definitely consider installing one. At the same time you can also make sure the guard pipe is clear of debris; having raised its cover, make sure you replace it securely. You could be liable

to heavy damages if a pedestrian were injured as a result of tripping over a cover that you had left open.

The service pipe stop-valve

The service pipe will run underground directly to your home. It should rise slightly as it does so to prevent any air bubbles being trapped, but it should be at least 800mm (2ft 8in) below the surface of the ground throughout its length. This is an important frost precaution. Even in the most severe winters experienced in this country, frost is very unlikely to penetrate as deeply as this into the soil. Make sure that you don't reduce this protection by, for instance, digging a drainage channel or creating a sunken garden above the service pipe.

Where the service pipe passes under the foundations or 'footings' of the house wall, it should be threaded through a length of drainpipe to protect it against any settlement which could fracture it. Generally it will rise into the home through the solid floor of a kitchen. Where, however, it rises through the gap between the oversite concrete and a hollow boarded floor, it must be protected against the icy draughts that may whistle through the sub-floor space. This is best done by threading the pipe, when it is first installed, through the centre of a 150mm (6in) stoneware drainpipe placed vertically on the oversite concrete and filling the space between the service pipe and the inner walls of the drainpipe with vermiculite chips or other similar insulating material.

It isn't, of course, practical to do this with an existing installation. In such a case the length of pipe in the sub-floor area should be bound with a 100mm (4in) thickness of glass fibre tank wrap or glass fibre roof insulating blanket, which should then be covered with a polythene sheet to prevent it from becoming damp and so useless as insulation.

A leaking service pipe

An underground leak may go undetected for a long period, but there are some tell-tale signs which should raise your suspicions. The main ones include the sound of trickling water when no tap has been in use in the house for a long period, a persistent noise from the main pipework, a loss of pressure in the flow of water from the cold tap over the kitchen sink, or a persistently damp patch on the garden path or on the wall of a basement. If you suspect a leak, contact the water authority. They have listening apparatus with which they are supposed to be able to fix the position of a leak. At least they can advise you on how best to track down the leak.

It is generally best to get professional help to deal with a leak in the underground service pipe. In an older house – where a leak is most likely to occur – this pipe will be of lead or iron which is difficult to repair. If the pipe is a modern copper one it will probably be leaking at a joint. To reduce the risk of this happening, water authorities normally insist upon the use of special manipulative (Type B) compression joints in underground locations. With these the pipe ends have to be widened

INSTALLING AN OUTSIDE TAP

1 *After turning off the main stop-valve, cut out a small section of pipe and insert a compression tee in the rising main.*

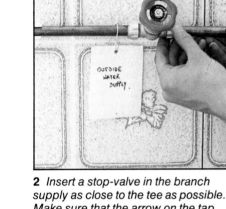

2 *Insert a stop-valve in the branch supply as close to the tee as possible. Make sure that the arrow on the tap points in the direction of the flow.*

3 *Work out where you want the branch pipe to emerge from the inside. Then working from the outside (or the inside) drill a hole through the wall.*

4 *Feed the branch pipe through the wall, then screw a backplate elbow in place just below it; this will act as the fixing for a new bib-tap.*

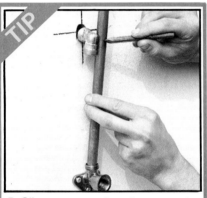

5 *Slip a compression elbow over the branch pipe and measure the length of pipe needed to reach the backplate. Cut and fit it in place.*

6 *Wind PTFE tape several times round the thread of the bib-tap. Screw the tap into place, making sure it is upright when you finish.*

– 'manipulated' – with a special tool as the joint is assembled. You may consider it better to replace the existing pipe with a single length of soft-temper copper tubing. This is obtainable on reels in long lengths that eliminate the need for underground joints.

Many water authorities nowadays also permit the use of black polythene piping. This too is obtainable in long lengths and has the added advantage that its thick walls help to insulate the pipe against frost. And in the unlikely event of the water within the pipe freezing, polythene pipe is sufficiently resilient to accommodate the expansion of the freezing water without bursting.

Putting in an outside tap

The only occasion when you are likely to need a permanent supply of water out of doors is when you put in an outside garden or garage tap. Before doing this you should

always seek the permission of the water authority. This is likely to be granted readily enough, but it will involve an additional charge on the water rate, particularly if you are going to use the tap for a hose pipe or sprinkler system. If you already have an outside tap you'll agree that the convenience of not having the garden hose snaking through the kitchen window, and putting the domestic water supply out of action while it is in use, makes this extra payment well worthwhile. Provided that your home has modern copper plumbing, fitting an outside tap is a straightforward job.

If the outside tap is to be fixed to the wall outside the kitchen, you will need a bib-tap with a horizontal inlet for outside water supply, with a threaded nozzle for a hose connector and an angled handle that you can turn without grazing your knuckles on the wall. You'll also need a 15mm wall-plate elbow

with a compression elbow bend, one 15mm equal-ended compression tee joint, a screw-down stop-valve with 15mm compression inlet and outlet and a length of 15mm copper tubing – how much will depend on the distance between the rising main and the new outside tap.

As far as tools are concerned, you'll require a couple of wrenches, a hacksaw, a tin of jointing compound, a roll of PTFE thread-sealing tape and some means of cutting through the wall to take the pipe-run outside. It's best to hire a heavy duty electric drill with hole-cutting attachments; the job can be done with a hammer and cold chisel, but this takes longer and is not as neat.

Turn off the main stop-valve and drain the rising main from the cold tap above the kitchen sink and, if there is one, from the drain-cock above the stop-valve. Cut the rising main at a convenient point to take off a

ADDING A SECOND TAP

1 Fit a 15x15x22mm compression tee into the existing branch. Use a piece of copper pipe to hold the fitting secure while it's tightened.

2 Fit the polythene pipe to the tee. Then clip it to the wall and take it down to a prepared trench at least 750mm (30in) deep.

3 At the other end of the trench, attach the second tap and a short length of pipe. Then run the polythene pipe up the foot of the post.

4 Link the polythene pipe to the copper using a 22x15mm compression coupling. Finally turn on the supply, check for leaks and back-fill the trench.

length through the hole in the wall. Connect the other end of the other length to the outlet of the new stop-valve.

Next you can go outside and cut the projecting pipe so that 25mm (1in) projects through the wall. Connect the other elbow to this so that its outlet points downward to the position of the new tap. Cut another short piece of pipe to reach the position of the new tap. Fit the wall-plate elbow to one end of this and connect the other end to the projecting elbow bend. Drill and plug the wall, and screw the wall-plate elbow into place. You'll then have to bind PTFE tape round the threaded tail of the tap and screw it into the outlet of the wall-plate elbow. If the tap doesn't point downwards when screwed fully home, you'll have to remove it and add washers to its tail until it does.

The job is now complete, apart from making good the hole through the wall with some mastic filler. With the onset of winter, turn off the new stop-valve and open the outside tap to drain the short branch to protect it from the risk of frost damage. There is no need to insulate the section of pipe on the outside wall.

Installing a garden standpipe

If you have a large garden, or a garage at some distance from the house, one tap fitted against the outside wall of the house may be insufficient, and you may need another standpipe to provide an adequate outside supply. This is an excellent opportunity to use polythene pipe for the water supply because of the long lengths in which it can be obtained. In fact, when new houses are built today this piping is usually chosen for all underground runs.

In order to install a second outside tap you have to carry out the preliminary work described above, but instead of fitting the tap into a backplate elbow, you can use a backplate tee. It is from the lower outlet of this tee that the additional garden supply is taken. You may not be able to get a tee of this kind to which polythene pipe can be directly connected. In this case fit a short length of 15mm copper pipe into the tee outlet and connect the end of the polythene pipe to it by means of a 15mm copper to ½in polythene compression coupling. However, probably the easiest method is to tee off the short section of supply pipe feeding the outside tap already installed.

Although polythene pipe will not be damaged by frost, it should still be laid in a trench about 750mm (30in) deep to avoid the risk of accidental damage from gardening operations. The pipe can be taken underground to any point required, and then connected to a tap fixed to a post or to the wall of an outbuilding by means of the usual backplate elbow.

feed branch pipe. If there isn't a drain-cock above the main stop-valve a little water will flow out as you do this, so be prepared for it. Make another cut 18mm (¾in) away from the first one and remove the 18mm segment of pipe.

Insert the 15mm compression tee into the cut pipe (described on pages 20 to 24) so that the branch outlet of the tee points along the kitchen wall in the direction of the position of the new tap. Cut a short length of copper pipe, say 150mm (6in), and fit it into the outlet of the tee. To the other end of this fit the screw-down stop-valve by means of its compression joint inlet.

There are two points to watch as you do this. Make sure that the arrow engraved on the body of the stop-valve points away from the rising main and towards the position of the new tap. Make sure, too, that the stop-valve handle is angled away from the wall so

you have enough room to turn it with ease.

The first phase of the job is now complete. You can turn off the new stop-valve and turn on the main stop-valve to check for leaks. Because this will restore water to the rest of the house you can carry out the rest of the job in your own time.

Drill a hole – sufficiently large to take a 15mm copper pipe – through the wall above the position of the new tap. When deciding exactly where on the outside wall you want your tap to be positioned, remember that you'll want enough room to be able to put buckets and watering cans beneath it. Then cut two more lengths of copper pipe, one long enough to pass through the house wall and to protrude by 25mm (1in) at each end, and the other long enough to reach from the new stop-valve to the hole that you have made in the wall. Join these two lengths with a compression elbow and push the correct